THE NO-NONSENSE
HOME ORGANIZATION PLAN

THE
NO-NONSENSE
HOME
ORGANIZATION
PLAN

7 WEEKS TO DECLUTTER IN ANY SPACE

Kim Davidson Jones

ROCKRIDGE PRESS

Interior Designer: Michael Patti

Cover Designer: Antonio Valverde

Photo Art Director/Art Manager: Michael Hardgrove

Editor: Daniel Grogan

Production Editor: Edgar Doolan

Cover Illustration: © 2019 James Olstein

Interior art used under license from © Shutterstock.com.
Author Photo: © Jama Finney Photography

ISBN: Print 978-1-64152-746-0 | eBook 978-1-64152-747-7

CONTENTS

INTRODUCTION AND HOW TO USE THIS BOOK x

PART ONE:
NO-NONSENSE 1

RULE 1: NO LONG LISTS 2

RULE 2: DON'T BUY ANYTHING YET 3

RULE 3: PARE DOWN FIRST 4

RULE 4: BE STRONG WHEN IT COMES TO SENTIMENTAL ITEMS 10

RULE 5: STORAGE SHOULD BE SIMPLE 11

RULE 6: LABELS COME LAST 13

RULE 7: ALWAYS KEEP SUSTAINABLE ORGANIZATION IN MIND 14

YOU'RE READY TO GO 15

PART TWO:
COMMUNAL SPACES 17

WEEK 1: KITCHEN 19

MONDAY: The Fridge 21

TUESDAY: The Freezer 24

WEDNESDAY: Mugs and Glassware 26

THURSDAY: Flatware, Large Utensils, and Dishes 28

FRIDAY: Pantry and Cabinets 31

SATURDAY: Appliances, Pots, and Pans 34

SUNDAY: Rest 37

WEEK 2: LIVING ROOM, PLAYROOM 38

MONDAY: Media/Bookshelves 40

TUESDAY: Shelf and Wall Décor 44

WEDNESDAY: Coffee Table 47

THURSDAY: Surfaces and Cabinets 48

FRIDAY: Kids' Media 49

SATURDAY: Kids' Toys 51

SUNDAY: Rest 54

WEEK 3: BATHROOM, MUDROOM, LINEN CLOSET 57

MONDAY: Bathroom Sink, Cabinets, and Drawers 58

TUESDAY: Shower and Cleaning Supplies 62

WEDNESDAY: Medicine Cabinet 64

THURSDAY: Hallway Linen Closet Shelves 66

FRIDAY: Hallway Linen Closet Boxes 68

SATURDAY: Mudroom 69

SUNDAY: Rest 73

PART THREE:
PERSONAL SPACE 75

WEEK 4: YOUR BEDROOM 77

MONDAY: Dresser Top 78
TUESDAY: Under the Bed 79
WEDNESDAY: Nightstand 80
THURSDAY: Drawers I 82
FRIDAY: Drawers II 84
SATURDAY: Closet 85
SUNDAY: Rest 91

WEEK 5: KIDS' AND GUEST BEDROOMS 93

MONDAY: Guest Bedroom—Drawers and Dresser Top 94
TUESDAY: Guest Bedroom—Under the Bed 95
WEDNESDAY: Kids' Rooms—Drawers 96
THURSDAY: Kids' Rooms—Toys 98
FRIDAY: Kids' Rooms—Under the Bed 99
SATURDAY: Kids' and Guest Room Closets 102
SUNDAY: Rest 105

PART FOUR:
STORAGE SPACES 107

WEEK 6: STORAGE CLOSETS, ATTIC, BASEMENT 109

MONDAY: Attic—Categorization 111

TUESDAY: Attic—Organizing and Decluttering 113

WEDNESDAY: Basement—Categorization 115

THURSDAY: Basement—Holiday Décor and
Miscellaneous Items 116

FRIDAY: Basement—Personal Items/Memories 119

SATURDAY: Storage Closet 120

SUNDAY: Rest 123

WEEK 7: GARAGE AND BACKYARD 125

MONDAY: Garage—Boxes 127

TUESDAY: Garage—Shelves 128

WEDNESDAY: Garage—Tools and
Cleaning Supplies 130

THURSDAY: Garage—Giving Everything
a Home I 132

FRIDAY: Garage—Giving Everything a Home II 133

SATURDAY: Backyard 134

SUNDAY: Rest 135

YOUR NEW HOME 139
INDEX 142

INTRODUCTION AND HOW TO USE THIS BOOK

HI, I'M KIM DAVIDSON JONES, owner of L+K Home Organization and mom to twins, Victoria and Dylan.

I have been an extremely organized person for my entire life. It was the way that I found peace and happiness, even as a child. My bedroom was my place of zen. My clothes were color-coded by style, my CDs were in alphabetical order by genre, and I started doing my own laundry in sixth grade so I could fold and separate my clothes the way I liked.

As I grew older and life got much busier, I somewhat lost touch with my organized side. It was there, but not as prominent. Then my world was turned upside down when I had twins. I was blessed with a boy and girl, Victoria and Dylan. The first year was a complete blur. We had everything under the sun thrown our way: My husband got a new job, the twins were in the neonatal intensive care unit for six weeks, and, oh, we decided to move . . . because, you know, why not? I was working seven days a week, with a side hustle on top of my nine-to-five corporate career, and just trying to keep my head above water.

As I looked around at all the boxes still not unpacked from our move, I realized that with my life as chaotic as it was, I needed to at least have my living space in order. So, the kids went to their grandparents' and the hubby went off to a boys' weekend. Before they even left the driveway, I had music blasting and everything coming out of boxes, closets, drawers, and any other area capable of being cluttered. This is how I spent the entire weekend, getting my home in a nice, peaceful, and organized state so I could easily find everything. No time to waste. At the end of the weekend, I finally sat down, completely satisfied and entirely rejuvenated.

It is amazing how great you feel when clutter isn't invading not only your physical space but also your mental space. I knew right then and there that I had to use my powers to help others, so that they could feel just like I did in that very moment: head above water, completely liberated. So, I walked away from my stable, secure full-time job of fourteen years to pursue that dream. I started L+K Home Organization to be able to go into homes and truly help others regain control. My goal is to be a resource for those who feel like they are drowning in stuff and spend their weekends catching up on housework, with little to no time for fun. Creating a sense of order and calm around an often-chaotic home environment allows families, couples, and individuals to focus on enjoying life instead of constantly stepping over it.

In my experience as a professional organizer I have worked with a lot of clients, heard a lot of stories, and had some tears shed along the way. Getting organized is not an easy task, especially when you have been holding on to items for years or even decades. Many times, clients know it is time to let go, but they just can't get there.

My very first client was an unpacking job in a new home. In my mind, this was a joyous and exciting occasion. However, the client was upset about relocating to a new city and leaving her dream home behind. When she walked into the new home and saw all her possessions there, she immediately started to cry. I wasn't prepared for that reaction and didn't know what to do. My answer was to stop everything I was doing and talk to her, ask questions. We discovered what items she loved and decided to unpack those first to make her feel at home.

I fumbled my way through that day and decided that would never happen again. Since then, I have read and researched as much as I could to truly understand the emotional side to getting organized. It can sometimes take an hour or two to let go of that first item; it isn't easy at all. However, the feeling of relief once you get started makes it all worth it. Plus, once you get going, it becomes like second nature.

On top of the emotional side, I have done a lot of research into how to sustain manageable organization. You wouldn't want to do all this hard work only to find that the results are impossible to maintain. Since this may seem like a very daunting task, I try to add humor and fun along the way.

Let me just say my home is by no means in perfect order. I am a mom who works full time, my husband has a very busy schedule, and we have two kids constantly running in different directions. The difference, however, is that I have set up systems in my home to easily put everything back in its place, even when it looks like a tornado just tore through the living room and stopped by the kitchen on its way out. My husband and I have set up scheduled times throughout the year (think Christmas or birthdays) to declutter and stay on top of all our stuff. This isn't just for the kids but for us, too. I will share all these tips with you as we go.

Before you make way for the new, it's time to let go of the old. We will dive deeper into this idea later in the book, but be prepared to "let it go," as Elsa from *Frozen* sings. Often, people will think that they need a bigger space, but generally the answer is much simpler than that; it's all about maximizing the space that you already have.

ALL SPACES

Getting organized isn't a one-size-fits-all approach. A family of six will have a very different style of getting and staying organized than a single millennial who is always on the go. The fundamentals of getting organized will be laid out in this book, but by all means customize this plan to do what works best for you. We will lay out tips and tricks for all spaces, from a home of 7,000 square feet to one of 700 square feet. Just because you have a large space doesn't mean you are organized; in fact, sometimes it means the total opposite.

If you don't have a garage, then you can breeze right through that section, or you can read all about it if you have a garage on your vision board for the future; the same goes for attics, basements, and backyards. For those of you who have inherited items from family members or are avid collectors, some of these sections may take you a bit longer. That is okay. There is no right or wrong, only organized.

THE PLAN

All right, time to get down to business. This book will walk you through a seven-week plan to get organized, no matter your situation or space. Breaking the steps down into small daily tasks makes the entire process far less daunting. Oftentimes, people want to get organized but get so overwhelmed they have no clue where to even begin, so they don't. If this is how you feel, rest assured you are not alone.

Also keep in mind that if you miss a day, that doesn't mean you have failed. We are all human, and we all slip from time to time, which is okay. If you do skip a day, set aside some time to make it up. I always compare this to maintaining a healthy eating lifestyle. It is okay to have pizza one day and enjoy the heck out of it; what's important is that you have the will-power and focus to get back on track. The very same is true for getting organized. If you have an event one night that you would really like to attend instead of working on your organizing, go and enjoy. Just note that you will need to add that evening's activity onto another evening or even extend the process out a bit longer.

The activities on Saturdays are usually a bit more detailed and time-consuming, because most people have Saturdays off. However, if your schedule doesn't allow for it, do what works for you. For example, my sister-in-law is a nurse who works on weekends. Her Saturday is really her Monday. So, she spends Monday— her day off—doing the longer activities. She also works three twelve-hour shifts in a row. She likely will not be able to tackle any activities after a twelve-hour shift, so she will combine a few days' worth of organizing into her days off.

No matter what your job is, you need a day of rest. Getting organized is no different in that regard. You need a day to relax and reflect on everything you have accomplished over the week, and we have set Sundays aside for that very purpose. You may even want to have people over to show off all your hard work.

This book is a road map to achieving your goals, so make it work for you. If you need to take an extra week for one section and make this an eight-week process, no one is going to judge you. If you get frustrated that it may be taking a bit longer, close your eyes, take a deep breath, and picture how amazing your home will look when you are finally done.

YOUR IDEAL HOME

The first step before we get into the thick of things is to visualize how you want your home to look. Imagine waving a magic wand and your dreams becoming a reality. What would that look like? How would you feel? Are you smiling just thinking of it? Write all of this down so you can refer back to it. I also recommend making a vision board. These seven weeks may feel long, and having something to look at to keep you motivated can be helpful.

Once you envision how you feel, then you can move on to the next step: getting started, one small area at a time.

These days so many people seem to feel that more is more. They must have the biggest houses, the large-and-in-charge SUVs, garages full of gadgets, and closets full of trendy clothes. However, do all these things really make them happy at the end of the day? Sadly, no. It is time to ditch the "keeping up with the Joneses" mentality. Heck, I am a Jones, and I can tell you firsthand, us Joneses are just regular Joes. Even we know having all that stuff isn't so great.

Have you ever thought about switching your mind-set to a less-is-more approach? This outlook is known as minimalism, which is an often-misunderstood movement of modern times. What is your first thought when you hear the word *minimalism*? A tiny home fashioned out of an old woodshed? A large white canvas with a single black dot in the center? Sure, these are modes of minimalism, but that doesn't mean they are the definition.

I always say I have a minimalist mind-set with a realistic approach. For me, that means I live in a

2,400-square-foot home, because I have a family of four plus a dog. My kids need room to explore and play, but at the same time they don't need to live in a toy factory. We continuously monitor what we buy and bring into our home, ensuring that we always have control over what exists in our space.

Your minimalist mind-set may be different from mine, which is totally fine. How do you envision your life and home with a minimalist approach? Does it mean less shopping, having fewer items lying around, having more time? It will look different to everyone, but the end goal is to be able to live a clutter-free life, physically and mentally. I always envision a life of creating more adventures and memories and having less stuff holding us back from doing so.

Another way to envision this: What can you see yourself doing in your space once it is organized? Can you see your children playing without stepping on Legos every two seconds? Can you see yourself pursuing the hobby you have always wanted to try but never had the time? You will be amazed by the time saved once you have an organized home.

This book will help you achieve all of the above. All you have to do is dream it and follow the steps, and it will become a reality. Please tell me you are smiling as you read this. I am smiling for you. In fact, I can visualize you reading the entire Harry Potter series in your tranquil bedroom like you have always wanted to but couldn't, because you could never relax long enough to get past page one.

PART ONE

NO-NONSENSE

AS MY parents always told me when I was growing up, rules are meant to benefit you. I strongly disagreed with that as a kid, but as an adult I've realized its wisdom. My job here is to hold you accountable, and to do so we need to set some rules in stone. These are not guidelines but hard-and-fast rules. Trust me, this will help you succeed. Adhere to these rules as much as possible, and you will ultimately find organizing success.

RULE 1:
NO LONG LISTS

You may be thinking, *Wait, doesn't this rule go against everything an organized person stands for?* Yes . . . and no. Lists are great if they are short and sweet, not daunting and overwhelming. Don't set yourself up for failure with a long list of to-dos for the day that you know you will not be able to accomplish.

I do my best thinking in the car at red lights, so I will jot down things I need to remember to do when I get home. I can just grab my iPhone and quickly put a to-do list in its Notes app. However, my lists are very short, made up of items I know I can achieve in the time frame I have to complete them.

Ditch the long, lofty lists, and use this book as the resource you need to get organized.

RULE 2:
DON'T BUY ANYTHING YET

People always seem to think that buying things will solve all of their problems. The first instinct is to buy anything and everything you see that says "get organized with this amazing organizer!" It is especially hard when you walk into Target and see all the beautiful displays, particularly the Chip and Joanna Gaines line. Even I struggle with that one and must put my blinders on when I walk by it. My mom has bought every single organizing product she has ever seen on commercials, but trust me, she is no closer to being

organized now than she was before. You already have everything you need to get started: an open mind, a vision, a plan, and, well, a garbage bag. Buying organizational items and bringing them into your home will only add to the clutter, which is the opposite of what we are trying to accomplish.

Yes, I know not buying stuff is hard, especially as you walk the aisles of your favorite store and all the cute shiny bins and baskets and containers call out to you. If you simply can't resist, then avoid places like this until you truly need organizational items, and when that time comes, have a plan and avoid overbuying.

RULE 3:
PARE DOWN FIRST

Rule 3 may be the most important, but it's also the one that gets me the most "Are you crazy?" looks. However, I believe that if you are going to do anything, you've got to do it 100 percent, and that means that before you get organized, you must pare down. To truly organize a space, you need to take every single item out of that space to evaluate what you have. Did you know that you have ten pairs of casual jeans? No?

Now that you do know, do you think you really need that many? Probably not. Keep what you use on a regular basis, and donate or toss what you don't.

As we work our way through the to-do lists in this book, we will walk through this process in every single room. While you're in the middle of paring down, it may look like you're making a bigger mess than you had when you started, but stick with it. I promise it will be worth it.

LET GO

On this organizational journey, we will start with areas where it will be easier to let things go, like the kitchen. Think about all of the items you obtained with good intentions but never actually followed through with. Mine was a high-end baby food processor. I wanted to become the mom who served only natural and organic foods to her babies. It was a fantastic idea, but then reality hit, and I realized I could buy jars of organic baby food at my local grocery store without having to take the time to make it myself. So much for the $200 appliance I thought I just had to have.

Do you have anything like this in your home? Did you decide one day to take up a hobby, go and buy everything, then decide you were not all that interested? It's okay; we've all been there. The important part is that you can now acknowledge that the hobby isn't going to happen and cut your losses. When you do, it will be easy to let go of anything and everything tied to that hobby.

Once you see the pile of items you've chosen to let go, you'll feel free, and everything will be much easier to let go of from that point on.

DONATING, SELLING, RECYCLING, AND TOSSING

The hard work of letting go is complete. Now what? It's time to determine what to do with all of it— whether the items should be donated, sold, recycled, or tossed.

Donating

Donating is a great way to give your items new life and let someone else enjoy them as much as you once did. It is always helpful to have a list of charities that you are passionate about, especially if they accept donations of clothing and household goods, such as Goodwill, Salvation Army, or Habitat for Humanity ReStore. I find it's easier for people to part with their items when they have places like this in mind.

An example of a good item to donate is a shirt you have worn a few times that is in great condition, but that you no longer enjoy wearing. Another example is a lamp you bought for your previous home that just doesn't work in your new home, especially if it's out of style and might be hard to sell.

Before you add an item to the donate pile, always ask yourself: *Would I like this if it were donated to me?* If so, it's likely a good candidate for donation. Then look at the item more closely. Does it have stains, rips, or tears, or does it barely work? If you can say yes to any of these questions, then this is likely not a donatable item. However, think outside the box. Your old towel may not be donatable for people to use, but the Humane Society and many other animal charities need items like these. Keep your furry friends in mind as well when donating items.

It is important to set timelines when donating items—that is, have a deadline by which you will drop off your donations. Otherwise you may keep putting off that trip to Goodwill until you forget about the items entirely. To help, I will remind you as we progress through your organizational journey.

Oh, and an added bonus—you may even be able to write off donations on your taxes. Check irs.gov for restrictions and rules.

Selling

To determine if an item is worth selling, put yourself in the buyer's shoes. Ask yourself, *Would I buy that?* Is it in good condition and useful? Does it still have tags? Is it still in the box?

A common mistake people make when selling items is putting huge price tags on them, either because of sentimental value or because of how much you paid for them originally. Do your research to understand what the market value of an item is before listing it for sale, and price it accordingly. In addition, develop a plan to either lower the price or donate an item if it hasn't sold within a certain time period—say a week.

If you don't have a lot of time, consider selling items at a consignment store. They will take a cut of your profits, so it's less money in your pocket, but it's still more than you had before you began the selling process.

Recycling

Did you know that as of January 2018, there are new recycling guidelines because China is no longer accepting "foreign garbage"? Take water bottles, for example. The bottle itself can be recycled, but the cap and little ring around the cap cannot. I had no clue. I recently discovered after watching a news segment that I was recycling items that actually couldn't be recycled. It was eye-opening to me, as it might be to you, so make sure to research before starting your recycling pile.

Tossing

If an item doesn't fall into your selling, donating, or recycling piles, it's time to toss it.

Most items have a life span, so don't feel bad about tossing something that has dutifully served its purpose for many years. A great example is an old sheet, or a floor mat that has been peed on multiple times by your beloved fluffy cat. (Bad cat!) No one wants that, and it is likely damaged beyond repair. Time to toss it.

RULE 4:
BE STRONG WHEN IT COMES TO SENTIMENTAL ITEMS

These will certainly be the hardest items to deal with, as they typically mean more to us than other objects.

I had a client who had kept a canoe his father had given him over 40 years ago. His property always had a lake or a pond nearby, yet the canoe never left his garage. He simply couldn't part with it because it was given to him by his father, and he had a lot of great memories of spending time in the canoe while he was growing up. However, the canoe was now becoming a burden as he had to have it moved thousands of miles across the country, and it was taking up space.

After we sat down and truthfully discussed why he was holding on so tightly to the boat despite never using it, we decided to take a picture of the canoe so he could always remember it—and then sell it to someone who would use and love it. It made him very happy to think of a young boy or girl getting to use it and make new memories.

You must dig deep in this area and sometimes ask yourself hard questions, but I know you can do it.

RULE 5:
STORAGE SHOULD BE SIMPLE

The goal in having storage is to make it as easy as possible to return items to their designated homes when not being used. The most optimal way to store items is by category, so you can easily identify what goes where. An example is to keep all snacks together in the pantry and then have another area for rice. One client I worked with decided that rather than categorize by rice, macaroni and cheese, quinoa, etc., she would have a section for side dishes. The categories must work for you, but keeping like items together is a simple rule to remember.

I will often refer to *overstock* throughout this book. Overstock is excess items you will want to keep in a storage space. This area is generally in the basement, garage, or attic, but it doesn't have to be. You can repurpose areas not being used for anything else for storage. An example of this is storing winter clothes under your bed during the summer months.

Also keep in mind that it is just as important for storage spaces to be organized as it is for personal spaces. Do you want a beautiful, organized kitchen that looks straight out of a magazine, but freak out if anyone opens a cabinet because all the contents will fall out? It's all about balance. Your mind cannot be free of clutter until your home is.

So, while you may think keeping the basement in complete disarray is not a big deal, it is. Your mind knows all of that clutter is there, and it will hold you back. Once, my basement flooded, and while I did what was needed to clean it out, I only did the bare minimum. Then life got busy, and I never got back down there. Every single time I had to do laundry in the basement, I would run down there as quickly as possible, shove a load in, and run out. It gave me major anxiety; often I would even avoid doing laundry if possible.

Then one week my in-laws were in town, and they were able to go down there and get the area completely organized. The difference was *amazing*. I felt physically lighter when I was down in the basement, and it was shocking how much laundry I got done.

"Go big or go home" is my motto. You are invested in getting organized, so don't stop until you get to the end.

RULE 6:
LABELS COME LAST

You must have a process and a system in place before you even think of whipping out the label-maker. My label-maker is one of my favorite tools in my work bag, but I always save it for last. In some cases, basic temporary labels may be called for throughout the process, but these shouldn't be any more involved than a Post-it note.

Labels need to be simple and must work for you. The point of labels is for everyone, even guests, to easily identify where everything belongs. If that isn't attainable, then it's time to look at the labels again. They may be too detailed and specific; if you have to think about what goes there, it slows down the process, and when there is confusion, items get left out and not put away. People can often go label-crazy and end up creating clutter because they put labels everywhere, rather than keeping things clean and simple.

RULE 7:
ALWAYS KEEP SUSTAINABLE ORGANIZATION IN MIND

The goal in getting organized is to create a system that you and your family can easily maintain. Take the time to set up these systems so you don't have to spend all your free time tidying up your home. You will even—*gasp!*—have spare time to go back and make areas look pretty and shiny, should you decide to do that. However, save that for the end, and keep your eye on the main prize, which is getting organized.

Remember that organizing your home is all about function. It doesn't have to look like a perfect Pinterest project. I decided one day for fun I would organize my kids' books by color. It looked beautiful and made for a great picture, but that was the end of that. My kids are not old enough to easily maintain the color-coding of their books. They can get the books back on the shelf, and that is good enough. My point here is: Create organizational systems that you know you can maintain.

In the chapters ahead you will be given the tools, steps, and knowledge to get organized in a way that fits your specific situation. Your organizational journey doesn't end after you read the final page. These tools will stick with you and grow as your life evolves.

YOU'RE READY TO GO

Okay, you know the rules, now let's hop to it. This will be a challenging seven weeks, but if it were easy you would have been organized years ago. Plus, the satisfaction you will have when this journey is complete will be a feeling like no other. And I will be right here with you every step of the way, to guide you through the process and provide all the tips and tricks for you to succeed.

Let's have some fun. Ready, set, go!

PART TWO

COMMUNAL SPACES

LET'S GET started with the communal spaces, which often are areas that have multiple purposes. An example is the living room—an area where you can decompress after a long day by kicking your feet up and watching TV. Oftentimes, it's also the kids' play area, a place to pay bills, even the location of an afternoon nap on the weekend. Maybe you live in an apartment and your living room also doubles as a home office. How do you make one space suitable for multiple functions?

First, less is always more. Do the kids need 5,000 toys? Do you really need 5,000 magazines that you hope to read? Should the coupons be lying in a pile next to the TV? The answer to all of these questions is no. In fact, having all of those items lying around will add more anxiety to your already stressful life. Physical clutter creates mental clutter. By eliminating the clutter, keeping what items you use most, and giving everything a home, you can truly enjoy the space and relax.

KITCHEN

The kitchen is very often the hub of a home. It's not only where your guests congregate, but it is also where you spend a lot of time. It is also one of the areas that has the most functions, ranging from a place to quickly eat breakfast before work to a place where mail goes to die in a large stack on the counter. By choosing to organize the kitchen first in your home, you are cutting off a main source of clutter and can find calm in an area you use every day. Also, it's best to start in a room where there are few items that pull at your heartstrings, like your favorite book or old love letters. Usually, we don't keep these types of items in the kitchen.

In the kitchen, we're going to start with the refrigerator. This will get your momentum going, since throwing out old food and empty mustard bottles takes no thought at all. Your "toss it" mind-set will kick in and prepare you for those more emotional areas to come.

Getting organized is not one size fits all. We don't all have large pantries or gourmet kitchens, and that is okay. Having an organized kitchen is less about the size of the space and more about its use. This is when you need to put all items out in the open, evaluate what you have, and then get creative and think outside the box when placing the items back in their new homes.

Many times we use vital cabinet space for items that are barely used. Can that item go into another area? Do we keep the spices on the opposite side of the room from where they are commonly used, leading to them being left out on the counter? To make the best use of space in a small or large kitchen, you must determine what each item is used for and the best place for it to call home.

Now, who's ready to get started with Week 1?

MONDAY:
THE FRIDGE, 20–30 MINUTES

> **MAKE SURE TO TAKE SOME "BEFORE" PICTURES (NO ONE HAS TO SEE THEM) AND THEN GET TO WORK.**

To get started, empty out the refrigerator and place everything into categories on the counter. Use categories that work best for you, but make sure to keep it simple. You can group drinks together, condiments together, and vegetables together, to name just a few.

Once you have your categories, look at each item and check the expiration date, or use the eye test for produce and veggies to see if these items have met the end of their freshness. Anything that has, gets tossed.

Have a garbage bag on hand that you can quickly take to the curb once it is full of trash. You may discover items in the very back of the refrigerator that you forgot you had, and they may not smell the best. I recommend a quick wipe-down of your fridge while you have a clean slate.

This is also a good time to evaluate what you keep purchasing but are clearly not using. I kept buying onions to use in recipes, but when it came time to use them, I would say, "Oh, next time." If I'm being honest with myself, I don't like onions and should just stop buying them regardless of which recipes call for them.

Once everything is grouped in categories and we have tossed all the bad items, let's start putting what's left back into the refrigerator. However, create a plan first. Where do you want to place the milk that you drink daily? Obviously, the back corner isn't the best place, so find a place that is easy to access. Be strategic, and make sure it is a good fit. Also, keep items in categories that make sense for you. I had a client who had an entire section on the top shelf of their refrigerator dedicated to morning items. This included everything needed to quickly get coffee in their hand before they had to tackle their day.

I have always found that fruits and veggies are best placed in drawers inside the refrigerator to extend their shelf life. Here's another helpful tip for the refrigerator: If you have kids who aren't big enough to reach the top shelf, place items like juice boxes and snacks on the lower shelves, so the little ones can help themselves.

A huge benefit of an organized refrigerator is that it'll be easier to find items when you need them; not only that, but it will also save you money on your grocery bills. How many times do you go to the grocery store and buy items because you think you don't have them, only to come home and find that you do? Being able to quickly identify what you have on hand before going to the grocery store will save you a lot of time and money in the future, so this is a critical step in getting organized.

TUESDAY:
THE FREEZER, 30–40 MINUTES

Usually freezers are not as large as refrigerators, but we try to cram just as much in them. Freezing items is a great way to extend their shelf life. But what good is frozen salmon if you can't get to it because it's jammed behind the bagged ice, push-up popsicles, and frozen vegetables?

You are going to hear this a lot because it is almost always step one: After you identify the area of the freezer you are going to tackle first, take everything out of that space. The second step is to put everything into categories and then identify what needs to be tossed or kept, just like you did for the fridge. The same guidelines apply: If it's too old or won't get used, it goes in the trash. Another thing to watch out for is freezer burn; if you notice that nasty ice forming on the food, you might want to toss it.

When placing items back in the freezer, try to use the "first in, first out" (FIFO) approach. This means you should use the items that have been in the freezer the longest before using items just purchased. Also keep in mind as you place items back in the freezer that meats usually take up a large area and can be expensive. Rather than continuing to buy chicken and steak every time you're at the grocery store because you aren't sure if you need them, group these items together in the freezer to be able to quickly evaluate what you have on hand. This is also helpful because you'll have a mental inventory before going to the store, and if there happens to be a huge sale and you want to stock up, you can quickly decide if you have the space to do so.

After you wrap up the freezer, give yourself a pat on the back. Let's now look on the outside of the refrigerator. What do you have hanging there? Cards, art, magnets, and reminders? Often this surface becomes cluttered—and it's right in your face every single time you open the fridge or freezer.

I recommend keeping little to nothing tacked to the fridge. One postcard from your favorite vacation destination, one piece of kids' artwork that is switched out periodically, and maybe a calendar—that is it. If you don't believe me, try it. I swear it will set the tone of peace and calm before you ever even get to the fridge.

MUGS AND GLASSWARE,

20–30 MINUTES

As we move into this next task and are no longer dealing with perishables, make sure to set aside an area for your donating, selling, recycling, and tossing piles. Make it as accessible as possible, while still being out of your way. If you have empty boxes, three of those would come in handy for this.

This next task may seem very straightforward, but it can easily get a little murky, so let's prepare for that. Mugs and glassware can represent memories or gifts from someone. Think about the mugs from college or that old travel mug from your trip to Key West. In the moment, they make for great souvenirs, but they can really pile up when added to your other glassware. Be prepared to part ways with some of these as you go.

Now that you have two days under your belt, I am sure you know how to get started. After you have everything pulled out and separated into categories, let's evaluate what you have on hand.

If you are tight on space, keep only the glasses and mugs that you use daily. Keep the extras—the ones you'd use for guests—in an area that is easy to access when needed but doesn't take up the limited space you have.

How many mugs, glasses, and cups do you use daily? How many do you have in total? Do you entertain? These are questions to ask as you sort through all the mugs and glassware that you own.

Remember that the items that should remain in the kitchen are those you are utilizing, and not ones you feel you must keep for one reason or another. If you must keep it, then determine where it should go. Is it a mug that represents a fun time in your life? Would you like to see it daily on your desk as a pencil holder? Or is it something that you find yourself drinking out of often? Break all the traditional rules and just do what works best for you. A coffee mug can have 5,000 uses other than housing coffee.

When placing mugs and glassware back into the cabinets, put the ones you use daily on the lowest shelf. For me, the coffee mugs go on the lowest shelf because they're the first thing I grab every single morning. I am usually in a fog and just need to caffeinate. The next shelf is where I keep my daily drinking glasses. On the upper shelves, I place specialty mugs and glassware that are used for guests.

THURSDAY:
FLATWARE, LARGE UTENSILS, AND DISHES, 20–30 MINUTES

These should be easy to breeze through, and you need a day of ease after mugs and glassware. I don't know what it is about those, but trust me, I can get stuck there, too. My husband thinks I collect water bottles, which I don't . . . I just like to be hydrated at all times.

So, for this section, break it down into five- to ten-minute increments for each category: flatware, larger utensils, and dishes. Take everything out of the drawers and start to categorize them in piles on the counter. Start with flatware and larger utensils.

For flatware, I suggest separating by knives, forks, and spoons. If you have different sizes within those categories, separate by size as well. This will help tremendously when you are trying to find a fork quickly and don't have to dig through all your flatware to find it.

If you have fancy flatware that is used only for guests, keep that separate; we will want to store it in a different spot. If you have fancy flatware but have never used it, even when hosting guests, ask yourself, do you need it? This may be a good time to sell it.

Larger utensils can take up valuable drawer space, so closely identify what you really use and what is just a gadget you purchased on a whim because it looked neat. Also, if you have multiples of any item and there is not a need, go ahead and put the extra items into donate or sell piles for the week.

When you return them to their drawers, keep all flatware and larger utensils in categories—for example, a pizza cutter, a spatula, an ice cream scooper, etc. This will make it much easier to find items when you need them. Use dividers as much as possible between these items to avoid them all ending up in a heap.

Next up is dishes. My main tip here is to focus on function and not aesthetics. There will be times in our lives when we have six plates that we use daily but none of them match, and that is okay. When choosing where to store these dishes, place them in an area that makes sense to you. Make it all about convenience. When you're at the sink and want a plate, what side do you naturally go to? Put your everyday dishes there. If you have an entire dish set just for guests that you use only a couple of times a year or for holidays, consider placing these in another area to give you additional space. We will discuss this more in the section covering the basement, where I like to have an overstock area.

If you have an abundance of flatware, utensils, and dishes that are taking up space and you know you will not use them, donate them. There are a lot of charities that will gladly take these off your hands— and plenty of buyers who will be forever grateful for your generosity.

TIME TO SELL THE ITEMS THAT MAY BE WORTH SOMETHING AND TOSS OUT THE REST.

FRIDAY:
PANTRY AND CABINETS,

30–45 MINUTES

Happy Friday! You have almost a whole week of getting organized under your belt. That is a huge accomplishment.

Now let's get to the pantry and cabinets. Those of us who live in smaller apartments, have small kitchens, or live in older homes like I do, don't have pantries. But don't fret if you are pantry-less. You and your food can still be organized.

First, take the opportunity to go back and address anything you may have missed in the first few days. Hopefully, you nailed Monday through Thursday, but feel free to reassess if you still need to pare down even more and make more room in your cabinets, as they are the most common spaces to house pantry items for those without a pantry. For those of you who do have a designated pantry, we can get started.

If you don't have a pantry or have a very small pantry, that is no problem. Use any cabinet space you have available as your pantry. If you don't have any cabinet space available, time to get a bit more creative. Look for open vertical space: Think the back of a closet door if you have one near the kitchen or the wall leading to the basement if that's right off the kitchen. This a great area to add shelving or cabinets if space is available. You want to make it something that will work for you, so if you have the perfect closet but it is on the other side of the house or apartment, then you may want to consider other options. The chance of these items getting back to their home on a daily basis becomes diminished if you make it harder to do so. To get started, let's take everything out of the pantry and start to categorize. At the same time, check expiration dates. If something is expired, go ahead and toss that item.

Before you designate or identify where everything will go, see what you have, and group it all into categories. Then, start to create a plan for where you will put everything back. You will want your protein bars, rice, canned veggies, and anything else that you use often to be in an area that is easy to access. Other items, like baking ingredients or other things you don't use as often, can go on a higher shelf and not be as conveniently placed. This may seem really basic, but it is one tip that will go very far.

Small bins are a great way of keeping items separated and organized within a pantry. However, don't forget Rule 2—Don't Buy Anything Yet. Measure your space and be ready, but wait until the end of the organizing process for your shopping spree. You may even find some available bins around the house while you're working on other rooms.

IF YOU HAVE ANY ITEMS THAT NEED TO BE RECYCLED OR DONATED, GO AHEAD AND DO SO TODAY.

With the remaining time, let's look at the kitchen cabinets where you keep your cleaning products. Often, these are stored under the sink: You open the door, toss an item in, and shut the door as quickly as possible so nothing falls out.

The cabinet under the sink can be pretty over-whelming, but it's actually one of my favorite areas to organize. After you remove everything from the space, evaluate what you have and what you need in the kitchen. Often you will end up with five Windex bottles because you have zero clue what is under there. Consolidate like items as much as possible, then keep one under the sink. Give the others a home where they are best used, and put remaining items into an overstock area. Focus on the essential

items you must keep under the sink: dish deter-
gent, all-purpose cleaner, glass cleaner, appliance
cleaner, and trash bags. The only cleaning items you
should keep in the kitchen are ones that are used in
that space.

SATURDAY:
APPLIANCES, POTS, AND PANS, 60–90 MINUTES

You have officially dominated the kitchen and shown
it who's boss. Let's end Week 1 on a high note.

We will start with the appliances. This is where
you will address items like the coffee maker, toaster,
Instant Pot®, blender, food processor, slow cooker, and
hand mixer. Some of these items will need to stay on
your countertops, as you use them daily. I'm looking
at you, coffee maker—there is no time to spare in
the morning to get it out of a cabinet, plug it in, and
then put it away when you're done. Your goal is to
maximize not only your space but also your time.

Try to keep your countertops with as little on them
as possible, but note what you use daily and make
space for these items. If you use the Instant Pot®
every day, keep it on the counter. Give it a home that

is maybe off to the side, so your countertops don't look cluttered. Do what works best for you, always remembering there is no right or wrong. For the other appliances that you use only occasionally, I suggest putting these into your overstock storage area, as it is not critical for you to access them quickly.

Moving on, let's look at pots and pans. This category can be a bit tricky due to sheer variety; there are nonstick, cast-iron, stainless steel, and probably many more that I've never heard of. People often accumulate pots and pans and find it hard to get rid of the ones they haven't used in years, mainly because they are super expensive. Keep in mind, you are not recouping any of your money by having pots and pans that collect dust. Let them go. They make great donations. Trust me, there are a lot of people who would love to use all of your old pots and pans, even if they are no longer up to your standards.

First, of course, it is important to lay everything out and see what you need—and what you don't. You may have five pots of the same size and not even realize it. Crazy, huh? It happens to all of us. In categorizing the pots and pans, separate by size and function: keep smallest pots together, and then within that keep like pots (such as saucepans) together as well.

The skillets will be in a category of their own, as they serve a different purpose.

When placing these items back, try stacking the pots and skillets as much as you can, to save space. You will want to give them a home as close to the stove as possible. The lids for these can be somewhat tricky. If you have the space, stand them up and use an organizer to keep them in place. This will also make it a lot easier to grab the lid you need and not have to dig through every single one.

Look at everything you have accomplished in just one short week—you should be very proud of yourself. How are you feeling? Are you smiling as you look around? Do you feel calm? Like a weight has been lifted off your shoulders?

Before we call it a day, look around and see if any area needs some last-minute finishing touches. This is where you can let your particularities run wild. Should the coffee cups have their handles all pointing in the same direction? Should you put out a fresh, clean hand towel? Now that your countertops are free of clutter, should you give them a quick wipe-down to truly make them shine?

ONCE YOU HAVE MADE YOUR LAST-MINUTE ADJUSTMENTS, TAKE AN "AFTER" PICTURE AND ADMIRE THE IMPROVEMENTS.

SUNDAY:
REST

This is your day to reward yourself for a job well done. Have you thought about making brunch and inviting a few people over? Not only will you feel great and renewed in your space, but take note of how much easier making brunch will now be. Need a pan for eggs? No problem—you know exactly where it is. Do you have eggs? Yup, they are right there on the breakfast shelf in the refrigerator.

Take this day to truly enjoy and rest in your new space. We have a big week ahead. For Week 2, we will jump right into the living room and, for those of us with children, the dreaded playroom.

LIVING ROOM, PLAYROOM

Many times, the hub of the home is the kitchen, which is why we started there. However, don't overlook the other area in your home that sees a lot of traffic: the living room. This space can have multiple purposes. For some, it may be their den; for others, it may be a play space or TV room. While the name, size, and function will vary, the common theme is that it is the communal space where you congregate with family and friends or enjoy some much-needed alone time.

If you breeze right through this section because you have a smaller space, that is fine. Hop ahead to the next section, as you may need more time in another area. Also, the tips I share in this section will appeal to a broad audience with different dynamics and spaces, but will hold true for all. You just have to tweak them to suit your situation.

MONDAY:
MEDIA/BOOKSHELVES,

15-20 MINUTES

GO AHEAD AND TAKE A "BEFORE" PICTURE.

When you're sitting on your couch and looking at the focal point of your room, whether it is the TV, a framed picture, or something else, can you focus on that object, or are you getting distracted by wires, books, and DVDs everywhere?

Let's remove every single thing from your living room bookshelves, including books and anything relating to media, excluding décor items. Once they're removed, place all items into categories:

movies, CDs, books, etc. If you have children, take it a step further and separate between adult and children in each category.

When reviewing the categories, think about when you used each item last. Do you have a DVD from ten years ago even though you don't even own a DVD player anymore? While that may sound unlikely, it is more common than you think. Often it is because people just don't know what to do with things, or they feel guilty about letting them go. You already have your charity of choice in place, so problem one is solved if you decide you no longer enjoy an item and it is time to let it go.

Problem two may be a bit trickier, but it's still manageable. What is making you feel guilty? Was the item a gift? Was it from a family member? Now, ask yourself: Would the person who gave you this item be upset if it no longer made you smile and you decided to pass it along to someone who would get use out of it? Most likely, they would not give it a second thought, and neither should you. Let go of all the clutter you no longer want to see in the room where you want to relax.

When returning things, I suggest keeping children's books and other items on the bottom shelves so the kids can easily grab them. Keep categories separated when placing things back onto the shelves. In organizing the items, do what works best for you. I enjoy keeping all family members' books separated, unless there is an overlap. I keep my husband's Harry Potter series in a space separate from all of my fashion books. The books are in the same area but separated. I enjoy color-coding my books as well, because for me it's an easy way to identify what everything is. When my kids get to the age where they are learning their colors, this will be a fun way to incorporate learning into getting organized. My husband, however, is doing well if he gets the books back to their home. As long as he has everything on the designated shelf, I'm happy.

I recommend doing something similar for DVDs and CDs as well when placing them back into the cabinets. When I was growing up, back in the day of CDs, I would separate all of mine by genre and then put them in alphabetical order. For me, that 100 percent worked and I wouldn't have had it any other way, but it is a bit over the top for the majority of people.

If you feel you are up to it, maybe it's time to rethink that DVD and CD collection entirely. Chances are, your favorite movie is streaming on one of the popular platforms. And that CD collection of yours could probably be sold for enough money to pay for at least *one* month of Spotify.

Consolidate cords, too, while you're at it. Nothing is worse than trying to relax and seeing a spiderweb of tangled cords to get your blood pressure up. The best way to do this, as we've done everywhere else, is to take every single cord out. You will then want to identify what cord goes to what and then run all of the cords to their source again. If you have any ties for garbage bags, grab those and wrap them around the cords to keep them nice and tidy. Also, if you can hide the cords—by running them behind a bookcase, for example—do so.

TUESDAY:
SHELF AND WALL DÉCOR,

30–40 MINUTES

You know the drill: First, remove and categorize. You may want to get more creative with your categories in this section. Rather than décor as a general category, break it down to items that are for display versus items that get hung on the wall.

Shelf décor is meant to be decorative and not overtake the space. An easy way to know if you have too much is, when cleaning, to see if it takes you more time to move things than it takes to dust. Plus, who really wants to dust, anyway? Make it as quick and easy as possible.

I firmly believe it is a good idea to switch shelf décor items out every so often to give the space a fresh look and feel. The same is true for wall décor. Do you still love what is hanging above your mantel as much as you did when you bought it? If not, swap it out for that framed print you have stored in the basement. This doesn't mean you should be going on a monthly shopping spree to obtain new décor, just that you should keep the pieces you love and switch them up from time to time. It can be as simple as switching out pictures in your picture frames.

If you have a smaller space but use the area for multiple purposes, try to repurpose items for multiple functions. I have one client who used a decorative table behind the couch as a desk. When they have guests, they just clear the space and make it an entertainment area.

Gently used shelf and wall décor are great items to sell if they are in good condition. While your style has changed, someone else may still find that succulent to be crazy cute. With the popularity of Facebook these days, it is a piece of cake to snap a pic of an item and place it online for sale. You can usually even put it on your front porch and have the buyer pick it up at their convenience. It is beyond simple and becomes a bit addictive. When I switched out the hardware on my kitchen cabinets, I put the older knobs on Facebook and sold everything within five minutes.

One common mistake people make is to overprice their used items. They know what they paid for the item and want to try to recoup a lot of that. Keep in mind that the item is used, and it needs to be priced accordingly. My theory is that even if you get $10, that is a free lunch, and you would get no money at all with the item collecting dust in your basement.

If selling items isn't for you, check your local charities. Many furnish homes for people getting back on their feet. We have a local charity that will post "after" pictures with the goods they've collected, and my clients are ecstatic when they see their once-loved décor hanging in a new home. I had a client who had a ton of Paris décor—it was her favorite city. When she downsized, she no longer had room in her home for all of it. She knew she needed to let go of some of it, so she did. She then saw her décor being used in a single mom's apartment, and she had the biggest smile knowing it was being put to good use and someone else could love it as much as she once did. She will never, ever regret letting go of those items.

WEDNESDAY:
COFFEE TABLE, 15–20 MINUTES

The coffee table can acquire as much clutter as the kitchen table and counters. It often has a stack of magazines, mail, books, remotes, paperwork, etc. Paper clutter can be the most overwhelming because it easily builds.

Look at the dates of all the magazines. If they are more than three months old, why do you still have them? If they had articles you wanted to go back and read, do you think the coffee table, where people put their drinks, is a good spot to keep them? I am guessing the articles weren't that important, or you would have placed them in a safer area. If you have not touched them, then it's time to recycle. You had good intentions—high five—but the reality is you shouldn't keep things you will never get around to reading. Be real with yourself.

Do the same practice with mail and any paperwork lying around. The mail is likely 90 percent junk that should have been recycled when it entered the door, and the other 10 percent could be bills, which you might want to think about paying.

Keep this area as clutter-free as possible. The last thing you want to do is dodge things on the coffee table when you are trying to put your feet up and relax.

THURSDAY:
SURFACES AND CABINETS,

15–20 MINUTES

Let's imagine that it's the weekend, and you decide to have a game night with friends and family. How much fun would it be to play a fierce game of Monopoly? You open the cabinets in the living room to look for the game, and everything spills out. You dig through it all—other games, old books, magazines, bills (hope you didn't need those), toys, etc.—only to discover you have no idea where Monopoly is. On top of that, you now have a huge pile of stuff on your floor. Bummer.

To avoid this situation, let's clear the cabinets and make room for the items you cherish and use often. Don't just shove every miscellaneous item in there and shut the door. The same process as usual applies here: Take everything out of the space and categorize. When going through all the items, make sure to discard, donate, or sell items you have not used in years and that are only collecting dust. Since you will likely have several categories (magazines, books, games, etc.), make sure to add bins to your shopping list to keep everything divided and labeled, so you can know what you have and can grab what you need without digging through piles.

If you have a game area in your living room cabinets, use it for games only, and only for the ones that you have used in the last year. Mark your calendar to declutter this cabinet annually—Christmas is a great time, as you may get new games added to your collection around then. The same goes for DVDs, toys, blankets, or anything else you store in the cabinets.

IF YOU HAVE ANYTHING TO SELL, GO AHEAD AND DO THAT NOW. IF SOMETHING DIDN'T SELL FROM LAST WEEK, ADD IT TO THE DONATION PILE THIS WEEK.

FRIDAY:
KIDS' MEDIA, 15–20 MINUTES

Does your kids' playroom share the same space as your living room? If yes, read on to learn how to let the spaces mingle without either side feeling like the other has taken over. If not, enjoy your evening off, or look ahead to next week to get a head start.

Do your kids have their own DVD collection, books, iPhones, iPads, etc.? Kids will easily outgrow something they were obsessed with just a few months ago. You will want to schedule a time to go through these items frequently to see if the kids are over them, and donate or sell what they no longer use. For younger kids, you may want to set a time quarterly to check things, in addition to around birthdays and holidays. As your kids grow older, I always recommend going through everything on events such as these, when they receive gifts. You may also want to incorporate a time when school lets out for summer and they come home with everything from the school year.

Kids can get easily overwhelmed; pare down and categorize so they can quickly find what they are looking for and move on without a meltdown. If you have kids who are different ages, separate their items if they are into different books and movies. If they have common things they enjoy, you can keep these together, but I always find it will reduce (note I didn't say "eliminate") fights when each kid has his or her own section. For example, for the older child, break their items into categories: CDs, DVDs, video games, etc. Then, when placing them back in the cabinet, give all of their items a dedicated space separate from the other kids'.

TIME TO DEAL WITH THOSE DONATE AND RECYCLE PILES.

SATURDAY:
KIDS' TOYS, 45–60 MINUTES

There is a slide and a play kitchen in my living room. This isn't a bad thing. My kids need to be able to play and have creative outlets, and theirs just happen to be located in our living room. It is their main play area, and it is also our main area to chill. And I can't chill with toys flying at me. In fact, it makes me anxious. However, I want our kids to just be kids and have fun, without me walking behind them, freaking out over the mess. So how do we get the best of both worlds?

An awesome method to help with this is to rotate toys in and out every few months. It will keep their toy selection minimal and keep them interested in the toys they have, without having to buy more. I keep out the toys they are playing with currently, and the rest I store elsewhere. Then, at a later time, I put away the toys they were playing with and bring out a new selection from storage. As you switch in and out, it's also a great time to declutter and donate or sell the toys they have outgrown or just don't love anymore. Try to declutter before gift-giving holidays and birthdays. This will make kids appreciate what they receive more and make them more willing to donate their old toys to another child who can now enjoy their once-beloved toys.

The best method to declutter toys is the same as with any other items: Take every single item out of its place and lay it out in the open. While doing so, categorize each item—dolls, arts and crafts, games, etc. It is easier to let go of items if you realize that you already have multiples. For example, if you have several boxes of crayons and they use only one box, the others can be passed on to someone who will utilize them.

Many people may encourage you to declutter without your kids' input, but I recommend the opposite. Get their feedback on what they love and can't live without. Involving them in the decluttering process will help them make these same decisions for themselves as they grow into adults.

Once all decisions have been made—what to keep, donate, sell, recycle, or toss—it is time to place the items you and your kids choose to keep back in place. It is very important to put a lot of thought into this, because you want to ensure that everyone is happy and it's clear whose is whose. Did you put the older child's dolls next to the younger child's teddy bear and then hear "That's mine" and then "No, it's mine"? Avoid this at all costs. Have separate, organized spaces for each child's toys. If they have toys they both utilize, place them in another area of the room.

Everything now looks like a picture out of a book, but you and I both know this isn't reality. It is not fun to be scared to touch anything because you don't want to mess it up. Your kids especially should be able to take out their toys as they want them, play with them, and then—most importantly—put them back. The reason everything is systematically placed is to make it very easy and quick to put the toys back where they belong.

Also try setting clear boundaries for your children when it comes to playing with and returning toys to their correct spots. My kids aren't allowed to move to the next room until everything in their play area is cleaned up. This is an expectation that has been set, and even though they are only two years old, they get it. Yes, they attempt to test that boundary, but if you are consistent it will get easier and easier. It just takes a while for a habit to form. Some say it takes 21 days; others argue it can take 66 days. But if you can get them to clean up just one toy for a few days, then build to two toys, and so on, it will become routine. Before you know it, next month they will be cleaning up their entire mess.

Congrats! You have finished yet another room—fist bump. What is the first thing you want to do now? This is the time to finalize all of the little details. Does the couch look weird now that there isn't junk next to it? Move it wherever you feel it belongs and has the best flow. This is your space, and you need it to feel just right in order to completely relax after all your hard work.

> DON'T FORGET TO SNAP THE "AFTER" PICTURE NOW THAT YOUR SPACE IS COMPLETE.

SUNDAY: REST

On Sunday, take advantage of your organized and calming living room. Can you see yourself reading a book? Well, go for it. You don't have anything to do now that the space is complete, so grab that book and put your feet up. It's your time now.

Enjoy your day, but get ready for Week 3, when we will continue to whip that house into shape. Who's excited?

BATHROOM, MUDROOM, LINEN CLOSET

This is a critical week, as we will be organizing the areas you see first thing in the morning, which often set the tone for your day. You don't want your first sight of the morning to be clutter.

Another major reason to get your bathroom and mudroom areas organized is to simplify your morning routine. How many times have you had to sprint out the door because it took forever to find what you needed to complete your daily process?

It doesn't matter if you have a huge bathroom with double sinks or a tiny pedestal sink; all the same principles apply. Also, don't worry if you don't have a traditional mudroom—you almost certainly have a space that serves the same purpose.

MONDAY:
BATHROOM SINK, CABINETS, AND DRAWERS, 30–40 MINUTES

BEFORE WE GET STARTED FOR THE WEEK, TAKE A "BEFORE" PICTURE.

You want your bathroom organized in a way that is conducive to your process. If you're one of the many people who are on autopilot as they roll out of bed in the morning, you'll want your space to be as intuitive as possible.

Step one is to take everything out of the cabinets and drawers and remove everything on the

countertops. Group everything together into categories and narrow down what you need and don't need. Cosmetics can be a girl's best friend, but they can also be our worst enemy. Men can have a lot of moisturizers and shaving gear. When you really start digging, how many perfumes, body lotions, and nail polishes have you collected over the years? Many of these items have a shelf life and are not as good after sitting for a while. And if you haven't used it in the last six months, how likely are you to use it in the next six days? Get that trash bag ready, and start a donation pile, even if you think this will not apply to this area. Homeless shelters are in constant need of toiletries, so if you have extras, put together a donation bag.

I often go the extra mile with my categories and make subcategories. For example, I have the makeup category. But within that, I have makeup that I wear daily, makeup for a night out, my no-makeup makeup look, and makeup for when I am feeling a bit adventurous. These don't necessarily need to all go together, as they are not used in the same manner.

Once you have everything in categories, create a system so that everything you need in the bathroom is easy to grab and go in the morning. This will save time and reduce your stress level. To do so, visualize your routine and what you use daily, and use the top few drawers for these items. This includes toothbrushes, toothpaste, hairbrush, face wash, and cotton balls and swabs. I separate my top drawers or shelf space by oral care, face, and hair. If you don't have a lot of drawer space, utilize the cabinets and closet (if there is one), or get creative. You can purchase movable drawer containers (once we're finished, of course) or utilize more vertical space in the cabinets with stackable containers. Use every space that is available to you.

If you are sharing the bathroom with anyone, separate the space by person. Some people are fine commingling belongings, but I recommend designating a separate space for each person's items. You want to have a flow and process that is just yours. You may not think it is a big deal for your partner's items to be mixed in with yours, but visually that might make it hard to process what you have.

Once the daily items are placed back, walk through your morning process and make sure the flow works for you. If it doesn't, go ahead and make changes as needed.

The items that are not used daily can be put on higher shelves in the cabinet or in lower drawers, but keep them in categories. This will help you easily find these items, even though you won't need them all the time.

Try to keep as little as possible on the counters and around the sink. I keep hand soap and a couple of little containers for a week's worth of cotton balls and swabs, a toothbrush, and toothpaste—that is it.

If you do want to place items on the counter, make sure you have receptacles available, or add some to your shopping list. Having the right container means items can remain in their dedicated homes and not end up all over the counter.

Congrats on making your Monday a success. You are off to a great start for the week. Tomorrow morning when you get ready, pay attention to how much easier it is, and see if you save time. I bet you will.

TUESDAY:
SHOWER AND CLEANING
SUPPLIES, 20–30 MINUTES

For the shower, categorizing and condensing are the keys. To get started, take everything out of the shower and start to make categories. I am willing to bet you have two bottles of the same product. Combine the contents into one bottle and discard the empty one. While I value that last ounce, I value space more. Some showers can be very tight, and the last thing you want is to be bumping into things as the soapy water runs down your face. That is not a good way to get your day started. It will also be a rough start when you accidentally use body wash on your hair instead of shampoo.

Line the items up in order of use when returning everything back to the shower, and stick with the essentials: shampoo, conditioner, body wash, razor, shaving cream, face wash. Don't overload yourself with options. If there are times when you prefer to use curly versus regular shampoo and have space to keep both of those items in the shower, fantastic. However, if you have a small shower, don't hang on to items that rarely get used. The majority of us have extra time on the weekends to get crazy and grab the curly shampoo if so desired, but those are valuable minutes during the week.

Once the shower is looking great, let's move on to the cleaning supplies. Bathrooms are not super spacious rooms, whether you live in an apartment or a house. With that said, keep in the bathroom only the cleaning supplies you use there. You do not need to store the bleach in the bathroom unless you have a specific reason to use it there. Keep your cleaning supplies categorized so when you quickly need to grab the toilet cleaner, you can do so. Keep only one of each cleaning product as well—any excess items can go into your overstock area.

WEDNESDAY:
MEDICINE CABINET, 20-30 MINUTES

The medicine cabinet reminds me a lot of the spice cabinet in the kitchen because a majority of these items have a shelf life that isn't often checked. Can you say with certainty that you do not have a prescription from five years ago still chilling behind that mirror?

Before you say, "I don't have a medicine cabinet" and skip ahead, think about where you keep your medicine or items that would typically be found in a medicine cabinet. If it's not an area you have already organized, then go there and get to organizing. The principle below will work for you as well.

It is imperative that you remove every single item from the medicine cabinet or comparable area and place them into categories. In doing so, look at each label and see if the item is expired or if it is old and has been sitting for a bit. This is a time when you want to create subcategories: daily use versus as-needed. I'm talking about your vitamins versus the Pepto that you only need to take after a 2 a.m. trip to Taco Bell. Place the items that you take as-needed on the top shelf, and keep the lower shelves open for the items you take every single day so you can have them lined up and ready to go.

The most underutilized area, I find, especially in smaller spaces, is wall space. Don't forget about your vertical area when getting organized. Small cabinets can be added to any unused wall for some additional storage. But remember, no buying until we're done.

Other items I keep in the medicine cabinet instead of drawers are liquids that need to be standing up. But again, if it is something you use daily, make it convenient for yourself. A good example of this for women is eye makeup remover or any oils. For men, you may want to keep a razor and shaving cream in there if you have room. However, if you shave maybe once a month, that may not be needed. Use your space to fit your needs, first and foremost. Follow this process, but don't stay in the box of where everything "should" go.

THURSDAY:
HALLWAY LINEN CLOSET SHELVES, 15–20 MINUTES

The linen closet, like many other areas, can be a place where you just stuff everything when you aren't sure where to put it. The last thing you want is a peaceful, organized bathroom and a disastrous linen closet. Your nice and relaxing bath will be completely negated as you drip water on the floor while you try to find a clean towel.

For the linen closet, categories are going to be important. Keep a section for bathroom supplies and a section for bedroom supplies. Within those categories, create subcategories. Keep your towels, washcloths, and hand towels separate. While it sounds simple, it will go a long way and is often over-looked. Think about when you grab what you think is a bath towel and it ends up being a hand towel. Do you fold it nice and neat and place it back where it belongs? No, you are frustrated and toss it back in the closet with little care as to where it ends up. By separating these items, you will establish designated sections for everything, making the hunt for a towel that much easier. I suggest keeping bathroom items on a lower shelf and bedroom items on a higher shelf. You use bathroom items more frequently than extra sheets.

The same principal applies to bedroom linens. Keep a section for sheets, fitted sheets, blankets, and pillowcases. There will be a time where you just need a pillowcase (maybe you're picking apples) and don't want to dig through layers of sheets to get to it.

Try to keep only the essentials in the hallway linen closet: towels, sheets, extra toilet paper. A good tip if your linen closet is on the second floor of your house is to keep a fire extinguisher in it, so you have easy access to one in the upstairs area should you ever need it.

If you do not have a hallway linen closet, consider installing some shelves on an area of unoccupied wall space. Shelves provide a great storage option in an area that would typically go unused.

IF YOU HAVE ANYTHING THAT NEEDS TO BE SOLD, GO AHEAD AND KNOCK THAT OUT.

FRIDAY:
HALLWAY LINEN CLOSET
BOXES, 15–20 MINUTES

Today will be somewhat of a carryover from yesterday. If you have boxes in your linen closet, have they turned into collect-all containers? Take everything out and evaluate what you have on hand. Do you need these items in the hallway closet, or would they be better stored elsewhere in the home? Some items to keep here are first-aid kits and Band-Aids. These are critical items you should be able to access quickly.

This may be an area that is utilized as your makeshift "junk drawer" as well. We all have one, collecting all of the different items we have and need, but have no clue where they go. It is okay to have a collect-all box, but you still need to be able to locate everything in it. How frustrating is it to need a lighter for your calming scented candle and not be able to find one anywhere? Or when you need a battery for the remote to change the channel?

TIME TO TAKE ANOTHER LOOK AT THOSE DONATE AND RECYCLE PILES AND DO WHAT NEEDS TO BE DONE.

It is very important to categorize within the boxes and make use of all the space. The best way to keep items separate is to utilize dividers so the items don't mingle together and become a big pile in which you can't find anything.

SATURDAY:
MUDROOM, 45–60 MINUTES

You may be thinking, *Me? A mudroom? That'll be the day.* But haven't you always had a mudroom of some sort? Even in college, when I lived with six girls, we had a designated place for our keys, shoes, and bags. Although it was not technically a room, it had the same function as a traditional mudroom—perhaps we should call it a "mudspace" for the sake of inclusivity.

Take a moment now to think about what area of your home could be considered a mudspace. What you keep there will vary in size, but the same fundamentals hold true. For an apartment with a small entry, you may be able to use one of the walls in the foyer as your mudspace. You will need hooks to keep keys, purses, backpacks, jackets, and coats off the floor.

Any item that walks out of the door with you every day needs to go in the mudspace. If you switch out coats or shoes every single day, those will need to go into the closet. Keep only the bare minimum if you are tight on space or if you have multiple family members. A family of five will have many jackets, purses, book bags, and shoes, which can add up to a lot of stuff very quickly. Therefore it is important you use this space exclusively for what is needed.

Shoes that are worn often should stay in the mudroom, because you want to be able to quickly toss them on and get moving. However, this is not the place to keep those high heels you wore to one Christmas party or the heavy-duty boots you use only during blizzards. When it is time to go shopping for organization products, baskets are a great solution for shoes. It may be more pleasing to the eye for the shoes to be neatly lined up, but is this realistic? Do your kids, husband, wife, roommates, or partner kick off their shoes the second they walk in? Well, these are the people who are not, no matter what, going to take an extra five seconds to bend down and place their shoes neatly in a row; it just isn't in their nature. They will, however, toss them in a basket. The basket at least keeps shoes contained and out of the way—no more tripping over that pesky rogue sneaker. If you have many people in your house, feel free to have multiple shoe baskets. There can be a basket per person, a basket for casual shoes, a basket for dress shoes—whatever is the best method for you and your household.

Another critical reason to designate a mudspace is to establish areas for important items. This will save you a lot of time and anxiety in the morning, because your keys will always be in the exact same spot. Ever been on a frantic hunt for your keys when you are already late? It is a feeling of sheer panic that is best avoided.

The mudroom or mudspace is likely the first thing that you and others see when entering your home. You want this area to be calming (aka organized) as you enter. Think about coming home after a long day, walking in to clutter everywhere, and then tripping over a shoe. I am fuming just thinking about it. Remember this the next time you thoughtlessly toss something in the mudroom because you don't feel like taking it to its designated home.

The bathroom and mudroom are areas you don't hang out in, and usually your time in them is brief: shower, brush your teeth, out. With that in mind, they can sometimes be the areas that are the hardest to keep tabs on. You want to make sure the dedicated area for each item is something you can easily maintain, even on a day when you oversleep and are in a hurry. Does it take any longer to put the hairbrush back in the top drawer than it would to just leave it lying out? It shouldn't. You want to make it that easy. Monitor your process and flow closely in these areas, adjust if needed. Also, keep in mind that you want these areas to look calming when you walk in, so leaving everything out on the counter simply so it's easy to maintain isn't a solution.

TIME TO TAKE THAT LOVELY "AFTER" PICTURE.

SUNDAY:
REST

Spend some time in the space you have organized, and enjoy. How about a bubble bath? In the past, it may have been challenging to just lie in a nice, warm bath and relax because there was so much clutter in the space. You can now relax and not worry about all the stuff lying around that may be causing you stress or anxiety. You also have the time to light candles, play some music, and just take it easy in a warm bath rather than scurrying around the home trying to clean.

PART THREE

PERSONAL SPACE

PERSONAL SPACES are your own private areas of zen, serenity, and tranquility; your personal sanctuary, so you want to make them as clutter-free as possible to truly be able to retreat there after a long day.

If you've ever watched a home remodeling show, you know it's very common that the homeowner's vision for their bedroom is "hotel- and spa-like." Can you imagine why? Think about when you stay at a hotel. You walk in and just want to melt into all the pillows. There isn't anything to clean, fold, or hang; all you have to do is relax and cozy up.

The same can be true for your own personal space. Create your vision for what you would like your personal space to look like. Is it a place to get a good night's sleep? A place to read a good book and block out any stress from the day? Is it all of the above?

All the vibes you want to have in your space are likely the same feelings you want to provide in the guest and kids' rooms as well. You want to create spaces of peacefulness where they can feel calm and relaxed, without distraction.

YOUR BEDROOM

When you are busy and overwhelmed, the greatest feeling is retreating to your area of rest, an oasis from the chaos of real life. If you go to bed in a space full of clutter, it will interrupt your sleep—and on top of that, it will be the first thing you see upon opening your eyes in the morning.

This is your personal space: a place that you associate with regeneration and privacy. Let this be an area that looks and feels like a hotel room but is all yours, a place where you want to cozy up at night to read a good book or watch your favorite TV show. This is not a space for bills, paperwork, stacks of magazines, or any other clutter. The number one purpose of a bedroom is to provide an area for sleep, so if anything is taking away from that, it's a problem.

MONDAY:
DRESSER TOP, 30–40 MINUTES

DON'T FORGET TO SNAP A "BEFORE" PICTURE BEFORE GETTING STARTED.

What items do you want to have on your dresser? Pick your favorite pictures and decorative items that make you smile. These items can remain; the rest will need to go. The point of a dresser is not to display every picture you have taken in your life—it is to house your clothes. The top of it is an appropriate space to add a few items, but not clutter. The dresser top can quickly go from a lovely pedestal for your photos to a hodgepodge of old receipts, incense ashes, and aspirin bottles.

On top of my dresser is a picture I took with my grandma before she passed away. This is a picture I love to look at every morning. I do not want to live without it in my bedroom. The same is true for a picture with my family. The picture of me having a blast a few beers deep with friends on the beach isn't as valuable to me. I love it and don't want to get rid of it, but it belongs in a different spot.

If you keep jewelry on your dresser, keep it contained. It is best to keep only the items you use frequently here, like a beloved watch or a wedding ring, and the rest would be better in an area dedicated to just jewelry.

TUESDAY:
UNDER THE BED, 20–30 MINUTES

If you have enough room in your closet to keep winter and summer clothes, then try to keep the space under the bed empty. I would suggest using this area only if you are short on space. The reason for this is that often items placed under the bed are forgotten, and they ultimately end up collecting dust.

If you do need to use the space, make sure it is functional. Under the bed is a nice place to keep off-season clothes in clear, long skinny bins (add to shopping list if needed). When switching clothes out for the season, make sure to take everything out of the space and give the area a good dusting.

When putting items away for the season, keep everything categorized and organized. It may get chilly one night during the summer, so you'll want to know if that sweatshirt bin is under the head or the foot. By having items categorized, you will quickly be able to grab them without shuffling through every other section. Place items like this—items you may need occasionally in the off season—under the edge of the bed and other items that you likely will not need (e.g., long johns in summer) toward the center. Be strategic about your placement. Get hot easily? Better store those summer clothes somewhere you can reach.

If you have extra space, place items only on the edges under the bed. It gets harder to grab items if they are pushed to the center.

WEDNESDAY: NIGHTSTAND, 15–20 MINUTES

If there is ever an area to go the extra mile with the minimalist mind-set, this is it. Your resting mind will know if you have stuff piled right next it, making it difficult to go into relaxation mode. Your nightstand needs to be as peaceful as possible. Keep the items you need to grab without getting out of bed there:

a lamp, your phone (only if it doesn't distract you from your sleep), a good book, and maybe one picture or sentimental item that will make you smile as soon as you wake up.

This is not the place for your bills or mail. I have been to a lot of clients' homes where they stack their mail on their nightstand. The last thing you want to do when getting ready for bed is look at junk mail or bills, lest you dream of the credit card statements and heating expenses.

For the drawers of your nightstand, the same rules apply. You may want to place the remote in there at night after you turn the TV off. I always think of what is in the nightstand when you go to a hotel. You can always count on a Bible being in there (of course, in your case this is optional), but there is also usually a notepad and a pen. Sometimes when I can't sleep because something is on my mind, I will grab a notepad, jot down my thoughts, and then go back to sleep.

THURSDAY:
DRAWERS I, 20–30 MINUTES

Drawers are broken down into two days because they hold all of the clothes that do not go in the closet, which can be a lot. You've got socks, undergarments, bathing suits, T-shirts, and pants, just to name a few.

So before getting started, break up your drawers into two days. Most people will have more T-shirts than any other article of clothing, so let's start there. Much like mugs, the line between sentimental items and old raggedy shirts can get a little blurry. Sure, you had a great time on spring break in Cancun back in your college days, but do you really need to hang on to that T-shirt you won in the karaoke contest? Let's think about that as we, you guessed it, categorize.

If you are short on space in the closet or drawers, think about adding baskets or stackable bins to keep in the bedroom. But remember, hold on only to what you genuinely enjoy wearing. You should not be adding storage bins to keep clothes that you no longer wear.

Once you have sorted all of the shirts into categories (workout, sleep, casual, etc.), assess the situation. How many of each do you have? Do you really go jogging enough to warrant your having nine breathable shirts? What about the shirts you haven't worn in a while but still feel like you need to keep? Is it because you have memories attached to them? If so, move those to the storage space where you keep memories, and get them out of your drawers.

Use the exact same process with pants, shorts, capris, etc. Don't put any of these items back into the drawers until you have gone through everything and decided what to keep and what to let go of. This will give you a better idea of how much space you will need. There should be a significant amount of clothes that you are letting go of, unless you have kept a tight lid on your collection throughout the years. When placing the clothing back into the drawers, make sure that you are folding them carefully. Folding clothes tightly and compactly can save space.

GO AHEAD AND SELL ANYTHING YOU HAVE PILED UP FOR THE WEEK.

FRIDAY:
DRAWERS II, 15–20 MINUTES

Today, let's focus on everything else in the drawers, outside of shirts and pants. It's time to deal with the socks and underwear—how exciting.

Take all of your socks out and match them up with their partners. Any lone soldiers? If so, leave them out. I keep solo socks in the laundry area to see if their partners turn up in the next few loads. If it is riding solo for weeks and weeks, chances are the mate is lost (sorry, mate), and it is time to toss it out.

Underwear and undershirts are a little less cut and dried. You'll have to use your detective skills to determine whether these articles are in good enough shape to hang on to. Anything with holes gets tossed (or repurposed into dust rags), and anything that has slowly changed color throughout its 100+ wears can go as well.

After you're done deciding what to keep and what to toss, it is time to place them back into the drawers. Keep your socks and undies easily accessible; I find that the top drawer is the best place for them. You are wearing at least one of these items daily (hopefully), so you want them to be right where you can easily get them.

The items that you don't use often can go into a bottom drawer or even in the back of a drawer. You want to maximize all your space, so the back of the drawer is a great spot for things you need only a few times a year, like a bathing suit or Spanx.

> ARE YOUR DONATION AND RECYCLING PILES GROWING? THEN IT'S TIME TO CLEAR THEM OUT.

SATURDAY:
CLOSET, 60–90 MINUTES

This is the big dog and an area that causes a lot of stress to many. You may want to go ahead and get the music, coffee, or whatever else you might need ready, because you are about to dominate this closet.

Don't worry, you are in good hands. Closets are my all-time favorite area, so I am here with all the tips and tricks to make this work for you.

Since this is a big task, let's break it down into sections: clothes, shoes, and accessories. With that said, go ahead and take every single item out of the closet.

As you take each item out, place it into its respective category.

Once you have everything out of the closet, take a deep breath. You will likely feel totally overwhelmed, and that is okay. That is why we already have a plan in place. Start with clothes and go through everything to decide what to keep, donate, sell, or toss. Next, go through shoes. After that, go ahead and do accessories.

Now that you have pared down to a select collection of your favorite clothing, footwear, and accessories, it's time to start filling that hungry closet up. Again, we will start with clothes. What do you usually wear daily? Is it casual or dress? Whatever it is, that needs to be the first thing you see when opening the closet door. Go ahead and put these items back into the closet, keeping them in categories (shirts, pants, jackets, and so on).

Next up: What other clothes do you wear often? If your first answer was dress clothes, then this answer is likely casual, or vice versa. Those will come next. Give them a home.

Now, what clothes do you have left, and is there hanging space available for them? Are they dresses and nice clothes you wear only on special occasions? Do you need these items to be in your primary closet? Do you have another space for those? Could you easily see what you have if you were to add those into the closet?

If you cram so much into a closet that you can't see what goes where, you won't be able to keep it organized and will be in a constant battle. People will say "I have nothing to wear" more often when their closet looks like a department store after holiday returns, as opposed to when it is pared down and organized. There are a couple of reasons for this—of course, because you can easily identify what you have and decide without being overwhelmed, but also because you now have only items you truly love and want to wear.

If you are tight on space, the key is to use every single bit of space possible. Many times smaller closets just have the one hanging bar, or the "one-bar wonder," as I call it. With that, there is a lot of empty space underneath the hanging clothes that isn't being used. A solution for this is to add another lower bar for items that don't hang long, like pants. If you have a lot of items that hang longer, like dresses, then this may not work. If that is the case, add drawers in the space available under the hanging area. You can also add shoe storage if you have a lot of room. The goal with small closets is to not leave any idle space; use every square inch, and remember to go vertical if needed.

Next up, it's shoe time. A tip for shoes that aren't worn daily is to keep them in clear containers. This will preserve them a bit and keep the dust off. Plus, it makes them easier to stack, and it maximizes space.

Once the shoes are done, move on to the accessories: hats, scarves, jewelry, purses, etc. Place these back into the closet in open areas, but be strategic. Put items that are not worn or used frequently on the top shelves of the closet. Hats can be stacked and placed into bins or clear containers as well. Jewelry is best in a jewelry box. For long necklaces, use your vertical space, and hang those to avoid them getting tangled. If you have a lot of scarves, try not to hang them. Scarves can get bulky, especially when you have a lot of them. You want them to be streamlined and easy to find. The best method to store these is to fold or roll them and place them into baskets or bins.

Pot lid holders are a great way to store small purses and keep them separated. This is a fun and cheap trick. For your larger purses, get a Ziploc bag and fill it with paper towels or newspaper, then stuff the bag in your purse. It will help the purse stand up, keeping its form and also making it easier to see. When you switch purses, just pull the bag out of one and put it right into the next purse.

If you have extra time and want to get crazy, let's make the closet pretty. That could include color-coding, if that is something you can foresee maintaining. When doing the finishing touches, think of your closet as a display at a store. With everything nicely arranged, not only will you smile and feel oh-so-happy, but you are more likely to not mess up something that you find pleasing to the eye.

By following the above steps, you have created systems to maintain organization. The item you wore today can easily be put right back on the hanger it came off without much effort at all.

How do you feel now? Relieved? Satisfied?

Once the closet is complete, do a little dance, because you have accomplished a huge task and should be very proud of yourself.

Take note in the next few weeks of how much better you sleep and how much time you save in the morning getting dressed. It is a total win, on top of having a bedroom that's a calm and peaceful retreat. This is truly your sanctuary.

TAKE AN "AFTER" PICTURE AND TRULY ADMIRE THE DIFFERENCE BETWEEN IT AND YOUR "BEFORE" PICTURE.

SUNDAY:
REST

Schedule some time to relax in your new space. Maybe sleep in, now that your bedroom is clutter-free. Some of my clients will grab a chair and sit in their closet if it is a walk-in. It is such a peaceful feeling.

Rest and relax. Week 5 starts tomorrow.

KIDS' AND GUEST BEDROOMS

Now that you have your peaceful area to rest, you may as well give the gift of organization to your kids and guests. Kids need a lot of sleep as they grow and develop, so giving them a peaceful place to rest is important. For your guests, you want to have an inviting area so they feel right at home, almost as if they are staying in a five-star hotel. It is important to enable easy access to necessities, so they don't have to rummage through your items or ask you where the basics are.

MONDAY:
GUEST BEDROOM— DRAWERS AND DRESSER TOP,

15–20 MINUTES

TAKE YOUR "BEFORE" PIC, AND LET'S GET DOWN TO BUSINESS.

You want your guests to be as comfortable as possible, which includes unpacking their things and making themselves at home. A good tip for the guest bedroom is to have it prepped like you are renting it out on Airbnb. If you are tight on space and need the dresser for your own things, try to leave at least the top few drawers available for your guests to put away their items. Now is a great time to go ahead and take everything out, to evaluate what you have. If it lives in the guest drawers, it probably isn't all that important to you.

On the dresser top, you can keep items that guests will need during their stay. Clean towels and washcloths look nice folded and stacked here, or you can simply leave the dresser top bare, thereby letting the guests utilize the space themselves.

TUESDAY:
GUEST BEDROOM—
UNDER THE BED, 15–20 MINUTES

The last thing you want is for stuff to be sticking out from under the bed in your guest room, which can cause anxiety or, worse, stubbed toes. You want guests to feel at home in your house, but you don't want them to feel like they are staying in someone's room.

Under the bed in the guest bedroom should be used only if you really need the space. If you are living in a home without a basement, attic, or other storage space, then by all means take advantage. If you do have those storage areas, though, I would strongly recommend keeping this area clear. This way, your guests can easily slide their own suitcases underneath the bed.

KIDS' ROOMS—DRAWERS,

20–30 MINUTES

Time to play your favorite game: categorize. Break the clothing down into shirts, pants, underwear, pajamas, socks, and other.

Kids can grow out of clothes quickly, so it is important to categorize not only by type of clothing but also by size. For items kept in drawers, try to narrow it down to a size range the kids currently wear, like 18 months–2T. Sizes vary between brands, so keeping a range is always a good idea.

For the kids' rooms, I always keep a bin or basket labeled "outgrown" to easily have a place to toss something when it doesn't fit. Many times, you put it right back in the drawer and either push it to the back or try to put it on them again later. Get it out as soon as you know it doesn't fit.

Once you have gone through everything and know what you want to keep, time to put everything back in the drawers. You will follow the same process as

you did with your drawers, starting with socks and undies at top. I organize each individual drawer by size: smallest clothes all the way on the left, largest all the way on the right. This will save you a lot of time, because you won't have to pick through everything when they outgrow one size. You can just grab the size group and remove all of it from the drawer.

If your kids are old enough to dress themselves, make sure they can reach all the drawers. You may need to move socks and underwear down a bit so they can access them, and put items not used often in top drawers. As kids grow and develop, it is important for them to make decisions, but it is harder for them to make decisions if they are overwhelmed. Keep categories separate, and don't include a lot of items, so they can quickly process and make decisions. Dividers and labels will eventually come in handy with kids' drawers, especially so they can differentiate what they have. This will help with not only decisions but independence as they grow into adults.

THURSDAY:
KIDS' ROOMS—TOYS, 20–30 MINUTES

The majority of toys should be stored in a communal space, rather than the bedroom. It is hard for kids to go to sleep when they are surrounded by colorful doodads and knickknacks. Much like I banned mail and paperwork from your bedroom, I am also banning excessive toys from the kids' room. There are very few kids who will say, "Mother, I am tired of playing with these toys. I would like to go to bed now." If it were up to them, they'd play until the wee hours of the morning. You must control that decision on their behalf, by removing many of the tempting trinkets from their rooms.

YOU PROBABLY HAVE A LOT OF NICE KIDS' CLOTHES TO SELL, SO GO AHEAD AND DO THAT NOW. YOU MAY EVEN HAVE SOME CLOTHING WITH THE TAGS STILL ON. THESE ARE THE PERFECT CLOTHES TO SELL.

Take all the toys out of the space and categorize. Before returning items to their spaces, determine what toys should be in the bedroom to make it a peaceful area for your kid. Think of the toys they enjoy sleeping with, the ones they snuggle up to each night as you tuck them in. Do you read books to them every night before bed? Keep books that are used nightly in this space as well; a bookshelf on the wall will keep them organized and maximize space.

I suggest then choosing maybe one or two other toys for them to have in their rooms, should they want to spend time there during the day. The others can go to the toy storage in the communal space.

FRIDAY:
KIDS' ROOMS— UNDER THE BED, 15–20 MINUTES

While I am not usually a fan of keeping items under the bed, this is where I make an exception. Since kids grow out of clothes so quickly, it is a good idea to

have the next size on hand. You will want to be able to get to these items quickly, as your kids move into the next size. Keep them in bins under the bed, categorized by type and size.

Kids also have a lot of art projects they bring home; I keep these in a separate bin titled "artwork," which makes it easy to add their next project without it lying around to possibly get ruined. This is also a good area to keep a memory box for them that you can add to as you create memories. This would be separate from the art box and contain things like pictures, cards, a first lost tooth, etc. These items can be stored in your storage space, but I like to maintain them in the personal space, since kids accumulate these items a lot quicker than adults do. These items are what usually end up as clutter on a dresser or counters; being able to easily identify where they go will hopefully eliminate that issue and at the same time preserve all the memories.

YOU MAY HAVE BIGGER PILES THAN NORMAL TO DONATE AND RECYCLE, SO GO AHEAD AND GET THAT DONE BY THE END OF THE DAY.

SATURDAY:
KIDS' AND GUEST ROOM
CLOSETS, 60–90 MINUTES

Let's get started in the guest room closet, then move into the kids' rooms. Take every single item out of the closet and categorize. The guest room closet is often home to overflow; it can also be a place where clothes go to die because you couldn't decide what to do with them. You are now fully prepared to make decisions on what to do with them, so let's do this.

Before you are finished categorizing, do you need to add any of the overflow from your primary closet? This is a great place to store the pieces you don't wear often but still want to keep, like dresses or suits.

Once you have decided what's staying and what's going, start putting your clothes back into the closet, making sure to leave some empty space for guests. If you can't leave half the space open, then at least leave a third. You may not have the space available for half, which is okay. Place the personal items you have left back into the closet.

Other items you should keep in the guest room closet are extra blankets and pillows in case your guests feel that the bed is lacking in accoutrements of comfort. Aside from these necessities and your clothes, the closet should appear quite barren, inviting your houseguests to make it their own.

The kids' closets may take a bit longer, since you need to not only take everything out and categorize, but also check sizing. Many times, you will be shocked to find a shirt that no longer fits. That shirt is taking up valuable space. The closet should hold only sizes that currently fit your child. If you have items that are outside of that range or are for a different season, categorize these items and place them in the right spot under the bed.

If you are short on closet or drawer space, add stackable drawers to a section of the hanging area in the closet. Kids usually have fewer clothes to be hung and more to be folded, so this is a great way to take advantage of that space.

Once everything is categorized into type and size, figure out which items are worn most often. Kids are hard on clothes, so the dressier and nicer clothes are usually not worn as much as play clothes. Keep the clothes worn daily where they're easiest to grab from the closet. The clothes not worn as often can go to the back or side. As you put these items away, keep them separated by size. Dividers are an easy way to quickly identify what size is where, should your kids be in multiple sizes at any given time.

For infants and babies, who go through clothes even more quickly than kids, you may want to have a size range per season. An example: If the baby is born in January, you may want to have a collection of clothes in the closet that gradually gets larger for spring and summer. Once they grow out of the smaller clothes, you can easily grab them and take them to be donated or sold. Then have the next set of seasonal sizes prepared in a storage area, or under the bed if you choose to go that route.

Feel free to put any finishing touches on the room to make it a space that you and your kids love to spend time in.

ONCE DONE, MAKE SURE TO TAKE YOUR "AFTER" PICS.

Congratulations on tackling not one but two areas this week. You are getting good at this.

SUNDAY:
REST

How do you feel about reading a book with your kids in their new tranquil space? Or maybe reach out to some faraway friends and ask if they want to come spend a weekend in your lavish guest room.

PART FOUR

STORAGE SPACES

PREPARE YOURSELF: These next two weeks are going to feel like a steep hill at the end of a long bike ride. Storage closets, attics, basements, and garages are generally where all the excess items go that don't belong in the living or personal spaces of your home.

Everything you have done in the first five weeks has built up to this. Are you ready?

Even if you don't have a dedicated storage room, you can still focus on the area where you keep items for storage, wherever that may be—if you haven't already organized that area. If you have, then grab some champagne and kick up your feet. If you haven't, dig deep. The end is in sight, and what a relief it will be to have your *entire* home organized. This will set you apart as a true organization champion.

STORAGE CLOSETS, ATTIC, BASEMENT

Storage closets, attics, and basements can be areas where you shove things when you don't know what to do with them, so be warned: You may be digging through years' worth of delayed decisions. These are also areas where your collectibles and memories are usually stored, on top of holiday décor and over-stock items.

You will need to not only be prepared to tackle a lot of different items, but also mentally ready to pare down. This could mean letting go of every single stuffed animal you have ever owned, or at the very least making the tough decision about which ones still bring you happiness. (Sorry, Beanie Babies.) So, get the music ready and start the coffee brewing— it's time to conquer this mountain.

If you don't have an attic or basement, where is your storage area? Is it a closet? Focus on the area where you keep the items I just listed. It doesn't matter if the area is big or small—the same challenges and principles will still apply. This area may be even more challenging for larger spaces because you had more room to keep adding things—until you didn't. For smaller spaces, keep only items that are critical, and truly focus on the minimalist mentality. The answer isn't just to get an expensive storage unit; the answer is getting creative with your space and keeping only the items you need or love.

If you have only an attic or a basement, but not both, focus on the area you have, and break the week down into even smaller daily projects.

My parents' home burned to the ground after I moved out. Even though I wasn't living there, I had left behind all my yearbooks, pictures, diplomas, and anything else I had kept over the first twenty-five

years of my life. There are some items I truly wish I still had—but not many. My dad survived this fire, and having him in my life is something I think about daily, not my possessions.

There is your pep talk. Let's get to work.

MONDAY:
ATTIC—CATEGORIZATION,

15–20 MINUTES

> **DON'T FORGET TO TAKE THAT "BEFORE" PICTURE.**

While I know you are used to the drill, the attic and basement are going to be important areas when it comes to categorization. These are your catchall areas, so there will be lots and lots of categories.

I recommend bringing out the Post-its to temporarily label all categories. In doing so, you can streamline the process and not have to stop and keep asking yourself, *What category was that?* It will also identify what goes where, should you have someone helping you.

Pick an open area in which to drag everything out and make clear and defined categories. The attic is generally an area with sloped ceilings that can be hard to access and walk around in (also, spiders). If that is the case, leave up there only items that you do not need easy access to. Examples include family heirlooms, old family pictures, or items that were passed on to you by loved ones that you are not yet ready to part with.

Any time I think of the attic, I automatically think of Clark Griswold in *National Lampoon's Christmas Vacation.* He kept hiding presents from his wife in the attic and then found years and years of unused gifts up there, covered with mounds of dust. Due to the limitations that come with an attic, utilize this area only if you are short on space in other storage areas, especially if it is not well insulated. Heat rises, and you don't want all your items to be ruined by moisture or humidity. If you must use this space, make sure to invest in airtight storage bins and even dry packets to ensure all items are kept dry.

For today, let's focus on categorizing and then determine what categories should go in the attic and what would be best in the basement. For the items that you would like to move to the basement, go ahead and get those out of the space. Should you not have a basement, then use every square inch of the attic space to the best of your ability.

TUESDAY:
ATTIC—ORGANIZING AND DECLUTTERING, 15–20 MINUTES

Yesterday, the focus was all about creating categories in order to decide what to keep in the attic. Today is going to be a bit more challenging, because now that we have decided what categories to keep in the attic, it is time to go through each one to determine what to keep and what to donate, sell, recycle, or toss.

It is often harder to make these decisions when an item has sentimental value, especially if it was given to you. Still, you will need to ask yourself, *Why am I keeping this?* If it is an item that you are keeping simply because you feel guilty about getting rid of it, maybe you have another family member who would love it. Even though these items are in your attic and out of sight, it still weighs you down when you keep something out of guilt and not happiness. Remember that.

Many times, my clients do not even know what is in their attic space. One of my clients recently bought a modern condo in a great location in an effort to downsize and simplify her life. Her previous house had two attics, over 3,000 square feet, and several acres of land. Her vision for the future was to be able to live in a space that required less upkeep in an effort to spend more time focusing on all of her hobbies.

In discussing our plan of attack, the first area she wanted to conquer was the two attics. Even though they were completely out of sight and out of mind, all of the stuff in that area was weighing heavily on her. It turned out the majority of the items up there had been inherited from her parents when they passed away. While she wasn't ready to let go of these items, she was able to identify what she had and organize it so that she would be able to access them when she was ready to use or let go of the items.

This may take longer than the allotted time, which is fine if you can skip another day that doesn't apply. If not, try to focus on time and try not to fall into the memory trap where you end up sitting on the attic floor going through every single picture and reminiscing.

WEDNESDAY: BASEMENT— CATEGORIZATION, 20–30 MINUTES

Be prepared to make what looks like a mess over the next three days. I have not lost my mind; stick to the process and trust me, it must look worse before it looks better.

First, we need a clear area to start categorizing. The two categories I want you to divide your items into are *personal* and *everything else*. Sound vague? Hear me out.

For *personal*, I am talking about items that are tied firmly to memories: pictures, letters, yearbooks, stuffed animals, trophies, etc. *Everything else* is any item that doesn't tug at your heartstrings, like holiday decorations and old paint. If you have items still in boxes even though you moved in a decade ago, take today to open every single box and remove all the items, placing those into categories as well.

This is going to take every single bit of 30 minutes, but you are accomplishing a lot and setting up the next two days to be successful. You may end the day tired, dusty, and sore, but visualize a beautifully organized basement in just a few days, and keep going. If a portion of your basement is furnished, follow the steps we utilized in your communal space (e.g., the living room) and for this section just focus on the storage areas.

THURSDAY: BASEMENT—HOLIDAY DÉCOR AND MISCELLANEOUS ITEMS,

20–30 MINUTES

Today, let's focus on the side of the room that doesn't fall into personal items, like holiday decorations and old paint. Go through each category to determine what to donate, toss, recycle, or sell. Break your categories down into even more specific subcategories, too, if they aren't clearly defined. For this, I mean separate holiday decorations into specific holidays. A fun tip I have found to keep these items organized and easy to grab is to line up the holidays by calendar year. Some people will even color-code the containers, but labels will work just as well—whatever makes it easier to know which bin contains which celebration. If you didn't use the decoration in the last year, does that mean it is time for it to go, or did you forget you had it?

Winter holiday decorations will likely be your largest category since these tend to be the most festive of the year; if so, consider breaking that category down even more, into ornaments, lights, tabletop decorations, etc. This will simplify the process when decorating, because you can bring one box out at a time and know exactly which area of the house it should go to. It also makes it much easier to take down decorations and put them away for the next year. I am not a huge fan of the winter holiday season, and I seriously think it is because it made my skin crawl when boxes and boxes of stuff overtook the living room each year with mass chaos. I might have a different perspective if everything was organized and easier to process.

Many people end up with years and years' worth of paint, even if the paint color is no longer in their home. This is probably because they have no idea how to dispose of it. Well, did you know that Habitat for Humanity ReStore will recycle old paint that is not dried up? They mix them with other paints and make fabulous new colors to sell, with proceeds going to the next Habitat for Humanity home. Not sure about you, but my mind was blown when I found this out. And since we've become such good pals over these past few weeks, I've got another little secret for you: For paints that are no longer good, mix them with some kitty litter—it'll soak up the paint, thereby making the can disposable. For the other paints you still need, make sure you label them to know quickly which one to grab for the next touch-up.

Go through each category to determine what to donate, sell, recycle, or toss.

IF YOU'VE FOUND SOME THINGS IN THE BASEMENT YOU CAN PART WITH, GET STARTED ON SELLING THEM TODAY.

FRIDAY:
BASEMENT—PERSONAL
ITEMS/MEMORIES, 15–20 MINUTES

Well, happy Friday. I purposely left the personal item side for last. You may need an adult beverage to make it through today, but don't get distracted. Break down the categories into subcategories, such as pictures, letters, and anything else. If you are part of a couple, I recommend keeping your memories separate, up to the time you met. My husband has decided to keep his childhood collection of a million baseball cards that he will *not* part with, even after I gave him multiple pep talks, so he has his own area. If I ever want to go grab a memory, it is easier for me to locate if I can go through just my items and not have these intermingled with my husband's things. Plus, his memories are not mine, so they don't hold the same sentimental value.

I do the same for my kids, so that once they are off on their own in the real world, I can give them their boxes of memories. If you had set aside items from personal or living space that you determined you had kept as memories (e.g., T-shirts or mugs), it's time to grab those and include them in this section.

After you have put everything into airtight containers and sorted by family member, I suggest storing these vessels off the floor. For many of us with basements, water is the main enemy. Items that are left on the ground are in danger of being ruined should the basement ever flood. When we first moved into our new home, I tossed everything in the basement and shut the door. We then got a huge rainstorm and almost everything was ruined, including pictures.

If you are choosing to keep these items, they must be special. Don't risk losing them to the elements.

If you need some more time to go through memories, add it on to your Saturday task.

> TIME TO DEAL WITH ANYTHING THAT NEEDS TO BE DONATED OR RECYCLED.

SATURDAY:
STORAGE CLOSET, 60–90 MINUTES

Storage closet can have several meanings here. It can be your only storage area if you live in an apartment or house without a basement or attic. If that is the case, hopefully you have already started working on this, since you found yourself unoccupied on the basement and attic days. If you took the week off, let's get to work now.

If you live in a home without an attic or basement, then storage is likely very tight for you. I recommend using this space wisely—that is to say, Costco may not be your best friend. Also, think of other areas in the home that have some spare room. Once you have gone through those and have seen what you have, evaluate if there is enough space and, if so, place some items there. Don't forget the ever-important vertical space. If you have a wall that's not being used, put some shelves there and designate that area for storage.

The other use I have for the storage closet is an overstock area. I have been dropping hints about this throughout the book, and hopefully you have put items aside that may need to go into this area. If you have no clue what I'm talking about, this is the area I use for items that are either bulk and excess or items I don't use often and need to place in an area outside of the main living space. This can range from the extra forty-five cans of green beans that mysteriously appeared in my grocery cart to the slow cooker that is used only for special occasions. I also keep platters and other items in this area that I maybe use once a year to entertain guests. You can add these items to containers to avoid the dust and spiders (chills just saying that word), but it is still not a bad idea to wipe down any items that were in the basement once you bring them upstairs.

The downfall of an overstock area is that it can quickly become a mess, thus negating the positive benefits of the area. You might go to the store and buy twenty rolls of paper towels when you already had several left. If they're on sale, stock up, but if not, save your space. I once went into the home of a family of six that had the perfect overstock area and even cute labels. However, it wasn't maintained and everything was just crammed in—there was no way of telling where anything was located. This defeated the purpose of the space, and they were buying items they didn't need.

When implementing an overstock space, separate it by area of the home—kitchen, bathroom, and bedroom—and then subdivide it from there: toilet paper, tissues, wipes, cleaning supplies. Anything of excess or that is not being used often, should be placed in this area to free up space in your living areas. This sounds like such a simple idea, but it will make a huge difference.

BEFORE YOU CALL IT A DAY, ADMIRE THE SPACES AND ALL YOUR HARD WORK, AND BE SURE TO TAKE A GOOD "AFTER" PIC.

SUNDAY:
REST

Now that you can easily find your memories from your childhood, sit in your organized space and go through all the pictures. Reminisce. Many people have their washer and dryer in the basement and will just run down there with blinders on to avoid the chaos, pop a load in, and run out. Imagine staying in the space and actually folding your clothes there, rather than taking them elsewhere because you just want to ignore the mess. Doesn't that sound so much calmer?

Not only can you now enjoy the space, but you should also be super proud of yourself for organizing an area most never get to. This is a *huge* accomplishment. Now rest up—time to hit the garage and backyard tomorrow.

GARAGE AND BACKYARD

The garage and backyard can extend out from the normal definitions: think anything outdoors. If you have a shed or veranda, group those in with these areas. If you live in an apartment and don't have anything outside of your living space, use this week to go back and put finishing touches on what you have done so far, get started on your shopping list to get what tools are needed, or give yourself a high five for completing this challenge.

Garages and carports can vary by size, but the main goal of these is usually to house your lawn items and your car. Many Americans have large garages to park their cars in, but cannot fit their cars into their garages because of all the stuff they have in there, taking up space. The same is true for sheds. How often do you give up on your garden simply because your weed eater is lost in the stack of random pool toys, empty propane tanks, and cobweb-covered coolers?

Since these tasks are going to mainly take place outdoors, ideally you want this week to fall when it isn't 20 degrees outside or, flip side, 100 degrees. However, if there's no avoiding the weather, plan for the elements and hustle through it. I cannot tell you how many calls I got one winter for garage organization, when people suddenly realized that having an ice-covered car made for a frustrating morning. I got out there in my parka and got to work, resulting in two cars parked in the garage. Boom.

MONDAY:
GARAGE—BOXES, 20-30 MINUTES

> **THE GARAGE IS THE ICING ON YOUR ORGANIZATION CAKE, SO YOU WILL NEED TO SNAP A "BEFORE" PHOTO.**

Let's get started. We will be spending the next few days sorting and categorizing, so if you park your car in the garage, plan on it being outside during that time. We will take advantage of the center space to spread everything out. If you can't fit a car in the garage at all, then we will need to take everything out to the driveway or surrounding area. In doing so, we will create space to put it back at the end of today's session so it isn't lying out on your yard or driveway.

The focus for today will be to take everything out of its box and place it into categories. You may have multiples or similar items, so don't go through anything until you have your categories complete. Don't forget the Post-it notes, as you will have a lot of different categories in the garage. Start with bigger ones (lawn-related, car-related), and then drill down into subcategories once you have everything sorted. If you come across tools or cleaning supplies, set those aside. We will tackle those on Thursday.

TUESDAY:
GARAGE—SHELVES, 20-30 MINUTES

You should still have all your categories in place from yesterday. Take everything off the shelves, if you have those, and start adding items from shelves to your piles. The same will apply if you have a shed or carport.

Now that you have everything categorized, start to pare down and decide what to . . . can you finish my sentence yet? Oh, yeah, you guessed it: Decide what you want to donate, sell, recycle, or toss. In doing so, you will determine what really needs to go into the garage area.

For those with small backyards—or just a balcony if you live in an apartment—think about what is most important to you in an outdoor space. Once you have a vision, create the space to fit that. If reading a good book is number one on the priority list, set up a small seating or lounge area. This may mean you need to sacrifice other uses, like dining or games. If you try to incorporate an area for everything, the area will be cluttered, making the space one you'll want to avoid no matter what.

Garages can sometimes be similar to basements—you toss something in there because you don't know what to do with it, and it ultimately just sits around collecting dust. Here are some items that are often found in the garage: lawn care products, lawn tools (mowers, rakes), outdoor chairs, outdoor toys, and tools.

If you find you have items that are outside of this list, think about why they are there. If you have a laundry area in the garage, then yes, it makes sense to have laundry-related items there, but if not, should you have a hamper chilling in the garage? I know you are thinking that sounds crazy, but trust me, I have seen it all.

The garage needs to be organized and functional, no different from any other area in the home. However, it is usually very last on your list of priorities, so it tends to get overlooked. You want to spend today paring down your categories and keeping only the garage essentials. If something has you stuck, put it aside to go back to tomorrow.

WEDNESDAY:
GARAGE—TOOLS AND CLEANING SUPPLIES, 20–30 MINUTES

Within the tools, make categories. If you notice that you have a lot of tools that belong in the home and your home isn't attached to the garage, would it make more sense for these to go into the basement or attic? If the house is attached to the garage and it's easy to grab a tool quickly, without putting on shoes or a coat, then it's okay to leave those as is. I'm not going to give too much direction on the tools, because everyone uses them differently, so do what works best for you.

Tools are expensive, and people have a hard time letting them go. For example, I have an ax in my garage that belonged to my husband's grandpa; it is old as heck but still does an amazing job of chopping wood. Don't forget that many tools make great candidates for selling. Eliminate the excess, and sell the tools not being used. Someone out there will be able to utilize something that you may consider old or outdated.

For the cleaning supplies, make sure they are products you use in the outdoor area or garage—for example, anything that you use to clean your car. Any indoor products will eventually land on the kitchen counter and likely stay there for a few weeks, so you may as well make a home for them indoors.

If you want to keep the auto cleaning supplies separate from other cleaning supplies, cool. You do what works best for you. My dad always kept window cleaner in the garage, but it wasn't for the glass in the home—it was to keep the dashboard of his car clean, so I would keep this with auto cleaning supplies. You don't need to stay inside a traditional box, but do keep items in categories. If someone were to walk into your garage, they should have a decent chance of knowing where to find a particular item.

THURSDAY:
GARAGE—GIVING
EVERYTHING A HOME I, 20–30 MINUTES

For the items you have decided to keep, let's determine where they fit best. Give everything a happy home.

Do you recall me saying repeatedly to use your vertical space? The garage is the champion and gold-star winner for vertical space. However, let's start with the shelves you already have.

What items do you not access a lot? This could be snow toys or other seasonal items that are not often used. Can those items go on the top shelves? The lower shelves need to be for items that are used more often. However, keep your pesticides, weed killer, antifreeze, or anything else that is toxic up higher. You want to make sure it is out of reach of kids and pets. In addition, keep these items out of airtight bins, to avoid any combustion in the heat. If you want to store them in containers, use open, clear containers so they can breathe.

If you have kids and they have toys in the garage, keep those on lower shelves so they can grab, play, and, most importantly, put everything back where it belongs.

FRIDAY:
GARAGE—GIVING EVERYTHING A HOME II, 25–35 MINUTES

For everything that doesn't go on the shelves, let's take a look at our wall space.

Do you have a pegboard? This is a super cheap way to keep things off the floor and hang your gardening tools. If you don't have a pegboard, a two-by-four hung on the wall with nails will have the exact same effect. If the item you want to get off the floor doesn't have a hole in it, get your drill out and make one. Easy peasy.

The goal is to get everything off the floor. This includes getting bikes off the ground, especially in the winter months if they're not being used. Hooks, specifically bike hooks, are a great, sturdy way to hang them.

For the items that must remain on the floor, such as a lawnmower, make sure you place them where you can easily get them out of the garage when needed. I would recommend placing them near the garage door on either the right or left side.

> TAKE EVERYTHING THAT NEEDS TO BE DONATED OR RECYCLED WHERE IT NEEDS TO GO.

SATURDAY:
BACKYARD, 45–60 MINUTES

We have made it to the outdoors and our last task.

The backyard is generally an area that the entire household uses, so get everyone involved and make it a family affair. What do you keep in the backyard? Due to the elements, you don't want to keep a lot of things out there. However, the grill, outdoor furniture, a swing set, a firepit, and other items of this nature (no pun intended) will, of course, all call the backyard home.

Categorize all the items you have in the backyard, and then let's get to work. What are essential items,

and what have become more like lawn ornaments? After you have categorized, it's time to pare down and decide what to donate, sell, recycle, or toss. Before placing items back in their designated homes, let's take a closer look.

Let's start with the grilling area. Grilling is a great activity during the summer months, to entertain outside or even have family dinners on the back porch. However, this fun activity can quickly become stressful if you can't find everything you need. This includes propane, grilling utensils, and the grill cover. If you keep these items with the grill, make sure they can be easily accessed when needed. Also, where is the grill in relation to the kitchen of the home? Often, you're bringing items prepared in the kitchen out to set on the grill. Is it easy to go back and forth? If the answer is no, let's move the grill closer to the house.

Next is the outdoor furniture and dining area. Do you have outdoor cushions that you move when it rains or gets cold? If you move them into the garage or carport, make sure that is close by and there is a designated area to keep these items. Another solution is to buy an outdoor chest (after you're done organizing, of course) that you can quickly toss the pillows into and take them out of as needed. Not only is this convenient, but it will preserve the integrity of the outdoor cushions. Your outdoor furniture and dining area must be inviting for guests and family to enjoy. If you have an average of six to eight people who use this area, don't overwhelm the space with more chairs. You can always keep extra chairs in your newly organized garage to grab if needed.

Once these areas are complete, move on to the toy section of the backyard. This may be the biggest area to tackle. I am a huge fan of playing outside as much as possible during the summer. The winter months can be long and gray, so once I see blue skies and temperatures in the fifties, out the door we go. The problem is that the backyard can quickly go from a lush green paradise to a disaster area littered with water guns, Frisbees, Nerf balls, and any number of outdoor toys.

That is why the best way to organize these is by activity type: sports, water play, etc. Then, once the kids are done with one activity, they can quickly put those toys back where they belong before moving on to the next activity. The best and easiest way to sort these items is with bins or baskets. When looking for this type of organizational tool, just make sure that it is outdoor-safe. If this is not possible, see if you can make space to house these items in the garage, and then bring them out to the backyard when play-time starts.

When I envision a backyard, I always think of the images in a home magazine. I picture a lush green space to eat burgers, sip some sweet tea, and enjoy the dusk lighting in a tranquil setting.

What is your vision? I'm guessing it doesn't include toys or debris littered around the yard. You want to keep very few items in this space and use it as an area to relax while enjoying the outdoors. Make it as easy as possible to return items to their dedicated homes every night before going inside.

DON'T FORGET TO TAKE "AFTER" PICTURES OF YOUR NEWLY ORGANIZED SPACES.

SUNDAY:
REST

This was your last and final week on a long journey. You deserve to celebrate. How about a stress-free barbecue with friends? Invite everyone over to come grill and dine in the newly functional and organized space. While guests are there, go ahead and open the garage door; let them admire how organized and amazing it is. Before, you may have avoided opening the garage door, too embarrassed by everything you had stuffed in there, but now you can open it up with pride.

Watch as your neighbors slow down to a crawl to gaze upon your accomplishment with envy. It is a huge victory to finish this last leg of getting organized.

YOUR NEW HOME

Congratulations on completing this seven-week organization journey. You should feel very accomplished and hopefully a bit more relaxed.

To maintain organization in the home, make sure that everything gets to its designated space every single night. It will take five seconds to toss all the toys back into their bins—but five hours if you let the mountain of toys build up over time. Pick a small activity to do each night to ensure that you stay on top of that nasty, invasive clutter. You could review the mail pile on Monday, straighten out your closet on Tuesday, etc.

I always compare organizational maintenance to doing laundry. Laundry isn't so bad to fold and put away when it is only a few items. However, when it gets to be stacks and stacks, it becomes overwhelming. You are less likely to accomplish this task because you don't know where to start. Instead, take five to fifteen minutes daily to tidy things up.

Also, once a new item comes into your door, determine what needs to happen with that item and then give it a home. This will eliminate the piles of clutter that sit around because you just don't know where everything should go. For holidays, like Christmas or birthdays, schedule time to review everything received and then determine if you need to declutter and eliminate old items to make room for the new.

To put the finishing touches on all your hard work, let's go shopping. Over the last seven weeks, I have reminded you to keep a shopping list of organizational tools you may need. If you haven't uncovered these items in your home, it's time to shop. Go into the store knowing measurements, items you need, your budget, and the purpose the items will serve. These tools will help keep items contained and in their homes.

I always prefer containers, bins, and baskets that match my décor well, so they serve both function and form. I want my pantry to be a lovely place that I enjoy seeing daily. Make your space pretty, and add your personality to the organizational tools.

The final touch, the icing on the cake, are the labels. Nothing makes me happier than seeing a beautiful area organized with labels that look like décor but serve a valuable purpose. If you aren't into fancy labels, then create or purchase labels that you enjoy. You could create an entire Pinterest board on labels if you wanted to.

Once you have completed these finishing touches, a great way to show off all your hard work and really put everything to the test is to have overnight guests. Take note, when they open a cabinet door trying to find a glass or bowl, how seamlessly they can find everything. They will feel right at home, and you won't have to worry about them opening a cabinet with an avalanche of junk behind the door. Enjoy the additional time you get to spend with your guests, rather than stressing over moving clutter out of the way.

Thank you so much for taking this journey with me. I hope you truly feel like a weight has been lifted off your shoulders—and that you can spend your free time enjoying life.

INDEX

A

Appliances, 34–37
Attic, 111–115

B

Backyard, 134–138
Balconies, 129
Basement, 115–120, 123
Bathroom, 57–58, 72–73
  cabinets and drawers,
    58–62, 65–66
  cleaning supplies, 63
  medicine cabinet,
    64–65
  shower, 62–63
  sink, 58–62
Bedrooms, 77–78
  closet, 85–90
  drawers, 82–85
  dresser top, 78–79
  guest, 93–95
  kids,' 96–104
  nightstand, 80–81
  under the bed, 79–80

Beds, under
  bedroom, 79–80
  guest bedroom, 95
  kids' bedrooms, 99, 101
Books, 40–43, 99
Bookshelves, 40–44, 99

C

Cabinets
  bathroom, 58–62, 64–65
  kitchen, 31–34
  living room, 48–49
  medicine, 64–65
Carports, 126. *See
  also* Garage
CDs, 40–43, 49–51
Children. *See* Kids
Cleaning supplies
  bathroom, 63
  garage, 131
  kitchen, 33–34
Closets
  bedroom, 85–90
  guest bedroom, 102–103

kids' bedrooms, 103–104
linen, 66–69
storage, 120–122
Clothing, 82–90,
96–98, 102–104
Coffee tables, 47–48
Cords, 43–44

D

Decorative items,
44–46, 116–118
Dishes, 28–30
Donating, 6–8, 46
Dressers and drawers
bedroom, 78–79, 82–85
guest bedroom, 94–95
kids' bedrooms, 96–98
DVDs, 40–43, 49–51

F

"First in, first out" (FIFO)
approach, 24
Flatware, 28–30
Freezer, 24–25

G

Games, 48–49
Garage, 125–126

boxes, 127–128
cleaning supplies, 131
giving everything a
home, 132–134
shelves, 128–130, 132–133
tools, 130–131
Glassware, 26–28
Guest bedrooms,
93–95, 102–103

H

Holiday décor, 116–118

K

Kids
bedrooms, 96–104
closets, 102–104
drawers, 96–98
media, 49–51
toys, 51–54, 98–99,
132–133, 136–137
under the bed, 99, 101
Kitchen, 19–20
appliances, 34–36
dishes, 28–30
flatware and
utensils, 28–30
freezer, 24–25

Kitchen *(continued)*
   mugs and
      glassware, 26–28
   pantry and cabinets, 31–34
   pots and pans, 34–36
   refrigerator, 21–23, 25

L

Labels, 13, 140
Letting go, 5–6
Linen closet, 66–69
Lists, 2
Living room, 39–40
   cabinets, 48–49
   coffee table, 47–48
   media, 40–44
   playroom, 49–54
   shelf décor, 44–46
   surfaces, 48–49
   wall décor, 44–46

M

Mail, 47, 81
Maintainability,
   14–15, 139–141
Media, 40–44, 49–51
Medicine cabinet, 64–65
Memory boxes, 101, 119–120

Minimalist mind-set,
   xix–xx, 110
Mudroom, 57–58, 69–73
Mugs, 26–28

N

Nightstand, 80–81

O

Organizational items, 3–4, 140
Outdoor areas, 134–138
Overstock, 11, 121–122

P

Pantry, 31–34
Paring down, 4–5
Playroom, 49–54
Pots and pans, 34–36

R

Recycling, 9
Refrigerator, 21–23, 25

S

Selling, 8, 45–46, 99
Sentimental items, 10,
   109–111, 113–115. *See
   also* Memory boxes

Sheds, 125–126. *See also* Garage

Shelf décor, 44–46

Shoes, 69–72, 88–89

Shower, 62–63

Storage closets, 120–122

Storage spaces, 11–12, 107, 109–110. *See also* Attic; Basement; Garage; Storage closets

Sustainability, 14–15, 139–141

T

Tools, 130–131

Tossing, 9

Toys, 51–54, 98–99, 132–133, 136–137

U

Utensils, 28–30

W

Wall décor, 44–46

ACKNOWLEDGMENTS

I cannot thank my family and friends enough for all of their support and contributions in helping me write my first book. They have allowed me into their homes to do research and practice, provided feedback on all my ideas, and even helped me edit. I am forever grateful.

During most of the time that I was writing this book, my mom was in the hospital, many miles away. There were times when I just wanted to drop everything and get on a plane to be with her. However, my family and friends (I am blessed with amazing girlfriends) pushed me to keep going. Not a day went by without texts and calls from them, often making me laugh and relax, and helping me remain focused.

The process of writing this book also has really made me grateful for what I have and made me realize even more that stuff can come and go, but family and friends are what's most important.

ABOUT THE AUTHOR

KIM DAVIDSON JONES is the owner of L+K Home Organization and mom to twins, Victoria and Dylan. She lives in Louisville, KY, with her twins; fur baby, Lilly; and husband, Ryan.

When she isn't busy helping others get organized, she enjoys spending time with family and friends, watching anything Bravo, being active, or enjoying a nice relaxing glass of wine!

You can connect with Kim on Instagram @lkhomeorganization or L+K Home Organization on Facebook. If you would like to sign up for the newsletter, to learn new tips and tricks, check out her website at www.lkhomeorganization.com.

CPSIA information can be obtained
at www.ICGtesting.com
Printed in the USA
LVHW010915020320
648657LV00001B/1